CONQUER
THE INFORMATION
MOUNTAIN

Also by Declan Treacy

Clear Your Desk!

CONQUER THE INFORMATION MOUNTAIN

Declan Treacy

Arrow
BUSINESS BOOKS

ARROW

Arrow Books Limited 1998

1 3 5 7 9 10 8 6 4 2

Arrow Books Limited
20 Vauxhall Bridge Road, London SW1V 2SA

Random House Australia (Pty) Limited
20 Alfred Street, Milsons Point, Sydney,
New South Wales 2061, Australia

Random House New Zealand Limited
18 Poland Road, Glenfield, Auckland 10, New Zealand

Random House South Africa (Pty) Limited
Endulini, 5a Jubilee Road, Parktown 2193, South Africa

Random House UK Limited Reg. No. 954009

Papers used by Random House UK Ltd are natural, recyclable products made from wood grown in sustainable forests. The manufacturing processes conform to the environmental regulations of the country of origin.

Companies, institutions and other organizations wishing to make bulk purchases of any business books published by Random House should contact their local bookstore or Random House direct:

Special Sales Director
Random House, 20 Vauxhall Bridge Road, London SW1V 2SA
Tel: 0171 840 8470   Fax: 0171 828 6681
www.randomhouse.co.uk
businessbooks@randomhouse.co.uk

Printed and bound in Great Britain by
Mackays of Chatham plc, Chatham, Kent

ISBN 0 09 927095 1

For Emily

Contents

Four Ates: sing the Information and Mond tax

CHAPTER ONE

Buried Alive

I get five different printouts with the same information from different departments. Since we got this new computer system I get stuff that I never received before. I just get the information because they have the capability to produce it.

We're buried alive under a mountain of paper! Don't take my word for it – the next time you get an opportunity, wander through your organization's offices and watch people at work. You will see your colleagues grappling with desktop stacks of reports, memos, faxes, computer printouts, manuals, standard forms and correspondence. If you look a little more closely, you will see that they are also struggling to cope with an avalanche of electronic paper in the form of e-mails, electronic reports and forms, and a mass of information downloaded from the 'net'.

The statistics will back up your initial observations. We have generated more information in the past 30 years than in the previous 5,000. In 1985 the volume of information in the world was doubling every five years – in 1994 it was doubling every nine months. In 1996 1,000 billion e-mail messages were sent around the world and by the year 2000 that number is predicted to rise to 7,000 billion. The amount of digital information in the world now surpasses the volume of information on paper (yet printer and photocopier sales are at an all-time high). Furthermore, the worldwide demand for office paper is increasing by 20 per cent each year. More than 1,000 books are published worldwide every day and a typical newspaper contains more information than the average seventeenth-century person would have come across in their whole lifetime. Our IT colleagues – while grabbing greater and greater amounts of the corporate budget – have been telling us that information is power but for many organizations the reality is beginning to hit home! The mass of information flooding our desktops is costly, time-consuming and deflects attention away from 'real' work. We've reached a crisis point and the frustrations expressed below by a long-suffering manager in a large financial institution could equally apply to all types of business.

Without really being conscious of it we're involved in two types of business. Our core business is providing a service to our customers and yet it seems that increasingly the energies of the organization are focused on a secondary business – paper processing. We waste huge amounts of time and resources generating, distributing, processing and storing reports, forms, memos, manuals, faxes, correspondence and other bits of paper. Added to that are the increasing quantities of virtual paper which are flooding people's desktops. While some of this paperwork is important, most of it deflects our attention away from the core business and adds no value whatsoever.

CONQUER THE INFORMATION MOUNTAIN SURVEY

A survey conducted for this book provides further evidence of the growing paperwork problem. Six hundred managers from 18 organizations were questioned about the volume of paper and electronic information passing across their desks.

These organizations ranged in size from 50–20,000 office staff and were located in five countries.

Survey results

- The volume of electronic information arriving on our desks is increasing by 20 per cent each year
- The volume of paper arriving on our desks is increasing by 8 per cent per annum
- 40 per cent of the information we receive is unnecessary
- Memos sent by e-mail messages are circulated on average to twice as many people
- 67 per cent of the e-mail messages we receive are junk
- We receive 18 items of junk mail a week
- Our colleagues send us 23 items of non-essential paperwork a week
- We spend five hours a week on non-essential paperwork
- Junk paperwork is always seen as somebody else's fault.

The survey shows that as office workers we are deluged with a growing quantity of information from both inside and outside the organization. Our desktop paper stacks are growing at a yearly rate of 8 per cent while our electronic in-trays are growing at a rate of nearly 20 per cent per annum. More than 100 documents land on our desk every week and even when unsolicited mail is excluded, 40 per cent of them are considered to be unnecessary.

The survey explodes the two great myths about office junk by revealing that the majority of the junk arriving on our desks is generated by our own colleagues and is in electronic, not paper format. When asked about junk paperwork most people immediately point the finger at unsolicited mail. The survey shows, however, that people receive more unnecessary paperwork from their own colleagues than from outside the organization. Every week an average of 18 items of junk mail in the form of trade literature, brochures, product manuals, order forms, customer surveys, leaflets, correspondence and magazines land on each desk. Our inconsiderate colleagues send us an additional 23 non-essential documents and this internal junk is a far greater problem because it can't always be ignored. If a marketing flyer lands on the desk, it can be binned immediately without any cost to the organization whereas if the chief executive demands a report which is never read, it is unnecessary but the work still has to be done. We spend an average of five hours a week generating and responding to unnecessary paperwork – the most common types of which are e-mail messages and bureaucratic forms.

Most of the junk we generate and circulate to our colleagues is in electronic format rather than on paper. All the organizations in the survey had introduced electronic mail and were disconcerted to find that it allowed people to circulate junk at a faster rate as well as valuable information. Sample groups of managers were asked to retain all their e-mail messages for one week and to classify them as essential or non-essential. (One person in the survey received 380 e-mail messages.) Sixty-seven per cent of e-mail messages were classified as non-essential because they told people things they already knew or things they didn't need to know. The A–Z of junk e-mail below illustrates the wide variety that circulates around our computer networks. Those surveyed also found that e-mail led to growing circulation lists, with people who might previously have been omitted being copied in on memos and reports. A sample of memos circulated before the introduction of e-mail was compared with similar electronic memos and the average circulation list was found to have increased from three to eight names.

For those wishing to declare war on paperwork the news is depressing. Of the 600 people questioned in the survey not one person believed that they were responsible for generating any unnecessary paperwork – they always blamed others for the mountain of excess information. This last finding is backed up by a survey carried out by the Institute of Manpower Studies looking at the effects of technology on personnel departments. Not surprisingly the survey showed that technology is enabling personnel departments to collect and disseminate an ever increasing quantity of information on employees. As a result personnel managers are churning out more reports than ever before. However, these reports were being generated without any consultation with the managers they were supposed to help. Of 200 managers surveyed nearly a third were dissatisfied or very dissatisfied with the type of information they received from the personnel department. The personnel managers interviewed were found to be focusing on 'the system' and were thinking of introducing more data and some were even thinking of a new system. Only a handful mentioned more communication with their internal customers as a future priority.

THE A-Z OF JUNK E-MAIL

Have you ever stopped to think about how much junk information is circulating invisibly around your computer networks? As well as increasing the efficiency with which you can communicate with others on important matters, e-mail allows your paperholic colleagues to generate and circulate more junk information than they ever dreamed possible.

A-mail   Avoidance mail – I don't want to tell him the bad news to his face so I think I'll put it in writing!

B-mail   Busy mail – your subordinates are not bombarding you with memos for your own good. It's their way of saying 'Look how hard I'm working. Look how busy I am!'

C-mail Cover your ass! mail – just in case there's a problem the sender has the documentation to point the finger at you!

D-mail Dead mail – the scores of memos in your electronic in-tray that you will get around to reading and processing some day, when you get the time – when pigs fly!

E-mail It's easy! It's electronic! It's exactly the same as paper!

F-mail For your information mail – lots of things you already knew or didn't need to know.

G-mail Gossip mail – 'Did you hear what happened to Sandra in accounts?'

H-mail Hate mail – 'It's all your department's fault!'

I-mail Indiscriminate mail – those bureaucrats believe that if they fire out information in all directions then someone is bound to find it useful.

J-mail Just in case mail – all those things your colleagues think you might possibly be, but never are, interested in.

K-mail Kamikaze mail – those personnel people are bombarding you with paperwork again.

L-mail Legalize mail – you've read it six times and you are still not sure what it's about. It sounds like it has been drafted by someone who has just swallowed a legal dictionary.

M-mail Me mail – 'Look what I've done, look at my sales figures for last month, I'm the greatest!'

Squawk! squawk! who's a pretty boy then?

N-mail Nuisance mail – that damned person in sales just won't leave you alone. That's 11 messages you've got from them today already!

O-mail Obese mail – 'As you can see from page 37 of attachment one, the procedure on page 115 of attachment two is invalid.' Help I'm drowning!

P-mail Pass the buck mail – 'I'm writing to let you know of my concerns about the forthcoming product launch.' Ha! I've just shuffled the problem from my desk to yours!

Q-mail Quick mail – It used to take head office three days to put together and circulate their junk memos. They can now produce dozens in the same amount of time!

R-mail Regurgitated mail – Hey! I've just sent that same memo to Jane and she's mass circulated it with her name at the top.

S-mail Social mail – 'Hi, John, what did you get up to over the weekend, buddy?'

T-mail Thunder mail – your temperature's at boiling point and you fire off a memo in a tantrum. 'That'll show him!' Re-reading your childish babbling later – 'Oh god, I wish I'd never sent it.'

U-mail Urgent mail – that blasted production manager marks all his junk e-mails urgent and it catches you out every time.

V-mail   Volley mail – here comes the reply to my message, back goes my response, the ball's in your court now, back it comes, a swift return, a forehand lob to the back of the court. Gosh is that the time! We'll have to continue this tomorrow.

W-mail   Withdrawal mail – Frank in PR is an e-mail junkie. It's more than 40 minutes since he last received an e-mail. The beads of sweat are beginning to roll down his forehead, his right hand is shaking. Phew! Just in time he thinks of something to circulate that will generate a response.

X-mail   X-rated mail – another secret rendezvous in the photocopier room is arranged!

Y-mail   Why mail – Why has he put it in writing? Why are you on the circulation list? Why can't he find something better to do with his time?

Z-mail   Zzzzz mail – you've been away from the office for three days and there are 150 e-mails in your in-tray. You're wading through them, your eyes are glazing over, you're drifting off to somewhere nice – a golden beach, palm trees, a refreshing cocktail, that beautiful person is smiling at you . . . 'BILL! BILL! WAKE UP! HAVE YOU FINISHED THE FIGURES YET?'

THE PAPERWORK BURDEN – ECONOMIC AND PSYCHOLOGICAL

You cannot run a business without paperwork. Where reports, correspondence, manuals, leaflets, newsletters, forms and memos help the business to achieve its goals then the documentation burden is an acceptable one. The problem lies in the fact that most organizations generate, distribute, process and store far more paperwork than is necessary to run the business efficiently. This non-essential paperwork is a huge drain on profits. Stationery costs, printing costs, photocopier and printer costs, filing costs and electronic paper costs will typically eat up 10–18 per cent of the organization's operating costs. And that's the good news!

These figures are dwarfed by the processing costs of paperwork. Research has shown that the cost of processing standard forms is 40 times greater than their printing costs, the costs of handling photocopies is 16 times greater than the cost of generating them and the cost of handling an e-mail message is 200 times greater than the cost of circulating it. The example below, taken from a local government organization that scrapped an unnecessary report, shows that the costs of handling it were 125 times greater than its stationery costs.

Stationery costs

20 pages × 18 recipients × 12 months
(4,320 pages per annum)   £100.00

Staff costs

	Hours
Gathering background data	2
Drafting	8
Proofreading and correcting	1
Printing	0.5
Photocopying	0.5
Distributing	1
Reading	12
Filing and Retrieving	1
Total	26

Payroll cost £12,480
(26 hours × £40 hourly staff cost × 12 months)
(£52 per page)

On top of the economic burden, paperwork imposes a psychological burden which has a similarly detrimental effect on the organization's profits. Technological advances were supposed to improve the quality of our working lives. However, highly stressed managers everywhere are suffocating as the gap between the information arriving on our desks and what we actually need to do our jobs, increases. Common sense tells us that we are unproductive when faced with heavy information loads. With a mountain of paperwork in front of us the important documents have less chance of being noticed or being acted upon. A recent Reuters survey found that almost half of senior managers say they are ill as a direct consequence of the stress that accompanies excess information. Two-thirds admitted it created tension with colleagues, hampered their ability to make decisions, decreased their job satisfaction and seriously affected their home life. Nobody can be blamed for their feelings of frustration, irritation and mistrust when they have to wade through piles of paper that should never have been generated. I recently attended a meeting where a manager in a healthcare organization suggested sending out a staff survey form to find out how people felt about their organization's paperwork. One of her colleagues, red in the face, jumped up and protested:

I'll save you the trouble – THEY HATE IT! They hate being showered with fat reports that have no relevance whatsoever to their function. They hate receiving bureaucratic memos telling them things they didn't need to know. They hate having to document their every action so someone else can check up on what they're doing. They hate filling in complex forms that ask for information they know is already available elsewhere. They hate being showered with 'cover your ass!' paperwork by people who have nothing better to do with their time.

THE PAPERLESS OFFICE – NEITHER ATTAINABLE NOR DESIRABLE

One of the main reasons why we are buried under this mountain of paper and electronic information is our obsession with achieving the paperless office. For the past 20 years organizations have been wasting huge amounts of time and money trying to make paper disappear into the computer. The paperless office however is not an attainable goal – computers, because they are attached to printers, allow us to produce more paper at a faster rate. Neither is it a desirable working environment because in many circumstances electronic documents are less user-friendly than paper. For a start the brain finds it a lot easier to take in the printed word than to decipher characters on a computer screen – that is why so many electronic documents are printed out before they are read. With longer documents the user-friendliness of paper is even more apparent. On computer a report remains hidden apart from the portion we have on screen whereas with a paper report we can immediately feel how heavy it is, skim through it to identify what the main headings are and zero in on sections of particular relevance. Furthermore as we read through the document we can highlight items or make notes in the margin – something that we can't do as easily with on-screen documents.

Through seminars and conference speeches I have long been arguing that organizations should stop seeing all paper as bad and all electronic information as good. Instead of concentrating on *how* information is carried we need to look at whether or not it adds value to the organization.

GOOD V. BAD PAPERWORK

Organizations thrive on good paperwork – it is clear, concise, timely, relevant and its pay-off is considerably greater than its processing costs. Unfortunately we spend much of our time dealing with bad paperwork – creating it, stacking it, sorting it, shuffling it, duplicating it, printing it, circulating it and filing it. Bad paperwork as illustrated below can be divided into four categories – Dead, Fat, Dump (distributed unnecessarily to many people) and Junk.

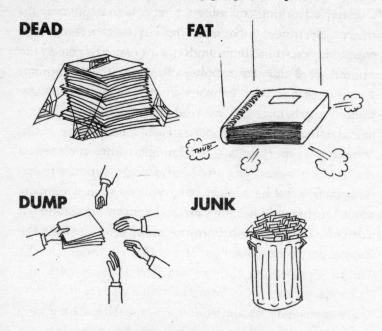

DEAD

FAT

DUMP

JUNK

Dead paperwork

Dead paperwork is any document that has passed its 'use by' date. It includes all the information hoarded on shelves, in filing cabinets and on computer disks that is no longer of any value to the organization – abandoned project files, piles of bumpf collected at exhibitions, old personnel records, sales literature that is years out of date, early drafts of reports, redundant forms and documents that have been retained beyond their legal retention schedules. Research has shown that about 85 per cent of the paperwork we file away will never be looked at again but we hang on to it nonetheless because – 'it cost money!'; 'it may become relevant in the future!' or 'we're going to look at it when we get the time!'

Dead paper files are a nuisance. They take up space in the office and we have to wade through them every time we are searching for something important. While dead electronic records are slightly less expensive to retain than paper there is still a significant cost involved not least of which is the cost of converting junk paper into electronic format.

A far more dangerous type of dead paperwork is that which is still being circulated throughout the organization, soaking up time and resources. It includes forms that collect information that is no longer used and procedures that once made sense but which now make the job more difficult to do. A participant on one of my seminars recounted the following horror story:

There's this one-page ad hoc report I requested a few years ago in response to a particular problem. I moved to a different office soon afterwards and I heard just the other day that the report, now 20 pages long, is generated monthly and a further eight names have been added to the circulation list. One of the people on the circulation list jiggles around the figures and regurgitates them back out to another bunch of people. As a result we have over 3,000 pages of junk circulating around the organization every year. I asked the report's author why it was still being generated and she was lost for words . . .

Fat paperwork

The second type of bad paperwork – Fat paperwork – includes any document that contains excess information.

Typical examples are bulky manuals, thick reports, long-winded memos and complex forms. Those who generate fat paperwork are often of the opinion that their verbosity impresses others but nothing could be further from the truth. Fat documents are an indication of lazy editing, poor organization of ideas and above all a lack of sensitivity for the needs of the recipient. While giving me a guided tour of his department one senior manager grumbled:

We could cut our paperwork by over 50 per cent if people were more concise. You can go through any in-tray in the building and you will find a bunch of memos that tell us in two pages what could have been said in two sentences. Any report less than 10 pages is considered to be incomplete and people try to outdo each other to produce the bulkiest volume. It hasn't really occurred to anyone that if we cut out the waffle then things would get done a lot quicker.

Dump paperwork

D.U.M.P. is an acronym for 'distributed unnecessarily to many people'. Dump paperwork includes all those multiple c.c. memos, mass circulation reports, forms that are passed from one person to another and all other documents which create complex paper trails. The paperwork may be relevant to one or two people and they can add value to it while everyone else is distracted from their work. One long-suffering IT manager I came across lamented:

The desks around here are c.c. dumping grounds – it's rare to receive an e-mail message with fewer than half a dozen names on the circulation list. When people compile circulation lists they should stop when they've included the one or two people who need to take action but they then add a few more names who they think should be kept in the loop, another couple of names are added so the boss and others know how hard people are working and finally a few more 'just in case' names are added.

Junk paperwork

The fourth type of bad paperwork, Junk, includes any document whose pay-off doesn't justify its existence. As we will see in Chapter Three when looking at bureaucratic myths, everyone who generates a document will vehemently argue that it is of value to the organization, but closer examination often reveals that their time would be spent more productively elsewhere. People find it easy to identify the Junk paperwork that others generate but have considerable difficulty in seeing that others might consider some of *their* outgoing paperwork to be junk. As one sales manager pointed out:

People become emotionally attached to paperwork that is part of their job and will come up with all sorts of rationalizations for generating it. My salespeople have to fill in lots of forms which are supposed to give senior managers a good overview of what's going on. That sounds logical enough but when one of my salespeople is neglecting a customer because she has to concentrate on internal paperwork it doesn't make commercial sense.

TOWARDS THE MINIMAL PAPER OFFICE

An environment in which all bad information has been eliminated can be described as a minimal paper office. The bureaucrats' cries about the lowering of business standards will be unfounded because just enough paperwork to get the job done well is generated. All that excess information which soaks up precious management time and deflects attention away from more valuable work has been eliminated. All documents, both hard- and soft-copy in the organization, will survive the bad paperwork test: is it Dead? (obsolete), is it Fat? (bulky), is it Dump? (relevant) or is it Junk? (low pay-off). In the minimal paper office information is not generated as an end in itself but as a means to getting a job done.

The route to the minimal paper office involves nine stages which are mapped out below. To complete each of these stages successfully requires what at first glance seems to be an inordinate amount of effort – after all 'it's only a few bits of paper!' However, the rewards in terms of huge cost savings, higher productivity and morale make the effort worthwhile. Furthermore the effort required to achieve the minimal paper office is only a fraction of what organizations currently invest in the white elephant of the paperless office.

The first stage involves conducting a paperwork audit to identify how much paper and electronic information is currently circulating around the organization. Stage two involves assembling a team of people to manage the organization's change from a 'paper-heavy' bureaucracy to a minimal paper office. Stage three involves constructing a plan that will serve as a road map for the changes about to take place.

The first three stages can be completed behind closed doors while the remaining ones are aimed at building support and commitment for the change throughout the organization. Stage four involves launching the campaign to create an awareness of the need for change. Stage five, creating a paperwork reduction exhibition, builds on this by showing people exactly how bad things currently are. Stage six involves holding workshops for all staff to educate, persuade and motivate them to move towards the minimal paper office. Stage seven involves a huge clearout of all the dead paperwork hoarded on the organization's desks, in its filing cabinets and on its computer disks. Stage eight, the paperchase, will leave no stone unturned in a bid to identify and eliminate all the unnecessary information and paperwork generated within the organization. The final stage involves reviewing the campaign and planning how to sustain the changes in the long term. The minimal paper office campaign should last for about 12 months although it should not be seen as just a one-office project but a permanent change in the way the organization does business.

The Minimal Paper Office Project

CONDUCT A PAPERWORK AUDIT

ASSEMBLE A PAPERWORK REDUCTION TEAM

PREPARE A PAPERWORK REDUCTION PLAN

LAUNCH THE CAMPAIGN

ORGANIZE A PAPERWORK REDUCTION EXHIBITION

HOLD PAPERWORK REDUCTION WORKSHOPS

ORGANIZE A CLEAR YOUR DESK! DAY

CONDUCT A PAPERCHASE

REVIEW THE CAMPAIGN

CHALLENGE BUREAUCRATIC HABITS

ADOPT PAPERWORK REDUCTION PRINCIPLES

In setting off on your journey to achieve the minimal paper office you should set a paperwork reduction target of between 20 and 40 per cent. This target provides a useful measure of how successful you have been in eliminating your colleagues' bureaucratic habits examined in Chapter Two and getting them to adopt the paperwork reduction principles discussed in Chapter Six. If you are prepared to be obsessive about eliminating unnecessary paperwork and information by tackling the bureaucratic culture in the organization then the information mountain can be conquered!

WHAT IS YOUR BUREAUCRATIC RATING?

The bureaucratic rating questionnaire provides a measure of how bureaucratic the organization's culture is – it is a good indication of how far away you are from the minimal paper office. Take a few minutes to think about the vertical flows of information in the organization between managers and their subordinates, the horizontal flows between departments, and the flows of information between your colleagues and those outside the organization. Then tick those statements that mirror how you operate.

Bureaucratic rating questionnaire

1 You can't get anything done without putting it in writing! ❏

2 We generate and circulate paperwork that should have been scrapped ages ago! ❏

3 We are often asked to provide information that is already available elsewhere! ❏

4 We are guilty of computerizing paperwork that should have been eliminated! ❏

5 More paper and electronic information is circulated than ever before! ❏

6 We generate as much junk internally as we receive from outside the organization! ❏

7 Paperwork is often circulated for the sender's

---

benefit rather than for the organization's good! ❏

8 We tend to adopt the 'more is better' approach
   when generating information! ❏

9 Documents that require action by just one person
   tend to be c.c.'d to several people! ❏

10 People always blame others for junk paperwork,
    never themselves ❏

11 Paperwork is often duplicated across different
    departments ❏

12 People become very defensive when their
    paperwork is challenged ❏

13 People circulate information without considering
    the burden it places upon others ❏

14 Our information and paperwork systems are
    becoming more complex over time ❏

15 Bureaucratic paperwork is a major contributor to
    low morale in the organization ❏

Bureaucratic rating 1–5

Your low score may indicate that you are well on the way
to conquering the information mountain – perhaps having
already run a minimal paper campaign. It is more likely
however that you have not been critical enough in completing the questionnaire. Paperholics like other addicts
have great difficulty in seeing that they have a problem and
that things need to change. You have been stuck in a bureaucratic mind-set for so long that you cannot envisage things
being done without mountains of accompanying paperwork. Successful bureaucracy-bashers say that it is only

when they look back after a successful paperwork reduction campaign that they can appreciate how bad things were.

Bureaucratic rating 6–10

While you are not as bureaucratic as many organizations the questionnaire will have highlighted many issues that demand your immediate attention. Don't lull yourself into a false sense of security by thinking that things aren't that bad – if you do nothing things will get worse! Seek out those in the organization who will support a minimal paper campaign and from a position of strength launch an attack on your bureaucratic colleagues.

Bureaucratic rating 11–15

You don't need a questionnaire to tell you that you are buried under a mountain of paper and electronic information. You and your colleagues are wasting huge amounts of time generating, distributing, processing and storing unnecessary documents. Morale is undoubtedly low throughout the organization with people feeling that they can't get anything done without filling in a bit of paper. The 'put it in writing' culture is so ingrained that you will face a high degree of resistance when trying to change things. Don't allow your colleagues to sabotage the war against excess paperwork with excuses such as 'it's the nature of our business' or 'there would be chaos if we got rid of it'.

What is your bureaucratic rating?

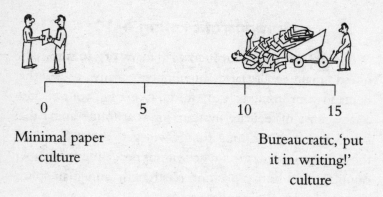

0	5	10	15

Minimal paper
culture

Bureaucratic, 'put
it in writing!'
culture

CHAPTER TWO

Bureaucratic Myths

'You can't take it away — it's part of my job!'

Bureaucratic myths are the excuses that people rely on to justify bad paperwork. In every organization these myths are used again and again until they eventually become accepted without question. Herein lies the reason for the dismal failure of most paperwork reduction campaigns. The focus is purely on the outward signs of the bureaucratic disease – paper – while the underlying cause of the information mountain, the 'put it in writing' mind-set, is left unchallenged.

Any attempt to apply common sense in eliminating a non-essential document will be met with one of the bureaucratic myths. Take the universally detested form that's been used in your organization for donkey's years – you know the one whose processing costs are ten times the value of the information it gathers. Suggest scrapping it at the next management meeting and I guarantee that one of your colleagues will cry aghast, 'We couldn't possibly get rid of it – we need it for legal reasons!' Alternatively, shake the dust off that manual on your shelf and suggest to others that as it is never used perhaps it could be scrapped. You can be sure that someone will summon up the full weight of their indignation and tell you 'That's a ridiculous suggestion, people won't know what to do if we don't have it in writing!' Each bureaucratic myth also has its own associated stories of the chaos and catastrophe that have ensued when the bit of paper was scrapped, 'in my last job,' or 'that I heard about on the manual-writing seminar I attended'. If you dig a little deeper, however, these excuses don't stand up and if the paperwork is scrapped or simplified the predicted problems never seem to materialize.

If the scale of the task ahead of you has not yet become clear, let me put it in plain English. Every Dead, Fat, Dump and Junk document in your organization will have a bureaucratic myth to justify its existence. To successfully conquer the paper mountain you will need to challenge and overcome hundreds or even thousands of them! Listed below are some of the most widely used bureaucratic myths. How many of them are used to justify bad paperwork in your organization? You will undoubtedly recognize most of them and be able to add many more of your own – the list is by no means exhaustive!

But I can't act unless it's confirmed in writing! ❏

But I have to put it in writing for legal reasons! ❏

But if I'm brief, people won't be able to make informed decisions! ❏

But if I'm not on the circulation list, I'll miss something important! ❏

But people ignore you unless you put it in writing! ❏

But if it's not written down, people won't know what to do! ❏

But other people need to know what's happening in my department! ❏

But I'd lose all control if I got rid of it! ❏
But it's only one piece of paper, it can't do any
harm! ❏

Myth: 'But I can't act unless it's confirmed in writing!'

Reality: Paperwork is not an essential part of the job!

You will know how frustrating it is to ask a colleague for assistance only to be told that nothing can be done unless your request is put in a memo or even worse, you fill out a form. Does the paperwork mean the job is done to a higher standard? Of course not! Does the paperwork mean the job is done faster? No, it actually slows things down! The paperwork is nothing but a bureaucratic intrusion and you could hardly be doing anything less valuable with your time! The only purpose for the paperwork is self-protection. Some time in the distant past a mistake was made, someone was shouted at and to ensure that they are never blamed again they insist on having the evidence in writing so they can pull it out and cry 'see, it wasn't my fault!' How many times a day do you and your colleagues play out the following scenario?

> *Bill*   We need help up here urgently! We're trying to prepare a presentation for a client tomorrow morning and the computer keeps crashing every time we try to print out the overheads.
>
> *IT Helpdesk*   Have you filled in the new computer services form?

— 31 —

Bill   The what?

Mary   The new computer services form. You need to fill it in and send it down to us. It's part of the new procedures we've introduced to make our department more professional.

Bill   But we need someone up here straight away!

Mary   Yes, just as soon as you fill in the form. Keep the top copy for your files and send the green and yellow copies to us. We'll keep the green copy on file and then get you to sign the yellow copy when the work is done.

Bill   Sounds very helpful! (Exasperatedly puts down the phone and goes searching for the form.)

Myth: 'But I have to put it in writing for legal reasons!'

Reality: You're suffering from an acute case of legal paranoia!

This is the most widely used and abused bureaucratic myth. There is nothing like the imagined threat of legal action to get bureaucrats busy generating paper. Every telephone conversation with a colleague is potential evidence in a future unfair dismissal case and every meeting with a customer will contain comments that will be relevant in a future court case. To be on the safe side everything must be documented.

BUREAUCRATIC MYTHS

'Bill Smith, you displayed wilful neglect in failing to document the telephone call you had with Susan in Personnel on May 28th. I therefore sentence you to…'

Bureaucrats will generate tonnes of unnecessary paperwork but claim that the blame is not theirs but that of the 'tight regulatory environment'. Organizations where this myth goes unchallenged will habitually generate and keep *thousands* of pounds' worth of 'legal' paperwork to avoid a potential problem that will cost them *hundreds* of pounds. Could the following conversation have taken place in your organization?

Records Manager   We call this area the black hole. We have tonnes and tonnes of paper in here. It's this new regulation that came in which means that if we don't have the information on file and the customer queries

	their records it could cost us up to £200.
Chief Executive	How much does this paperwork cost to keep?
Records Manager	The equipment and paper cost about £30,000 a year. However we're about to purchase a new computer system that will allow paperless storage and retrieval – it should pay for itself within three years!
Chief Executive	How many customers queried their records last year?
Records Manager	I have the information in this report here. Eh! it was eight in total.
Chief Executive	What is £30,000 minus £1,600?

Myth: 'But if I'm brief people won't be able to make informed decisions!'

Reality: Being brief involves cutting out the waffle not the important information!

Trimming the fat does not mean that you have to leave out important information. Try editing the memos that have arrived on your desk during the past week and see how much fat you can trim away without losing the meaning. Our educators are to blame for schooling us to produce fat documents. As children we were encouraged to produce no less than ten lines on what we did during the holidays and by the time we got to university it was 'write a minimum of 10,000 words on the following topic'. The message was drummed into us 'the more you write the more you know' with the emphasis on quantity rather than quality. Furthermore research has shown that academics give better grades to those who use big words and complex sentence structures than to those who say the same things in plain English! We can't be blamed for carrying those lessons into the world of work and thinking that thick documents look more impressive than thin ones.

It's not surprising then that a product manager who proudly showed off a report on one of my seminars was taken aback when it was suggested that this monthly masterpiece might be too weighty. A later conversation with his boss revealed the truth.

Product Manager   I know this report is 30 pages long but I couldn't make it any shorter without leaving out vital information. My boss is in a position of great responsibility and she can't make decisions on the basis of a couple of scraps of paper. Anyway, if I sent a short report to my boss she'd think I had nothing to say or that I whipped it up in no time at all. I spend several days a month researching this report and pulling together all the figures and I want my boss to know how much work I've put into it.

Boss   His reports read like a doctoral dissertation. To be honest with you they are so bulky that they tend to get pushed aside for later reading. Invariably they get buried and forgotten about under a pile of other stuff – I found two of his reports in the boot of my car the other day and the kids had scribbled all over them. I don't know how they got there and I can't remember ever reading them. He doesn't appreciate that I'm only in the office for a certain number of hours each day and that there's always a three-foot pile of other stuff to be looked at. If I see a brief report that I can digest in five minutes it's far more likely to be picked up than a wodge of paper that will take ages to go through. Even when I do pick up his reports and read them he's so long-winded that I lose concentration and miss the important points.

Myth: 'But if I'm not on the circulation list I might miss something important!'

Reality: Being on too many circulation lists deflects your attention away from what's important!'

You will often hear your colleagues complaining about being c.c.'d on too many things but when it comes to taking their name off circulation lists they become suddenly reticent. There is a fear that not being on the circulation list will make them less important or that one day the report they browse through every month will contain something useful. The more circulation lists we are on, however, the less time we have to spend in reading information that is directly relevant to the job. In many cases if our names were left off the circulation lists we wouldn't even notice.

Chief Executive	Do you remember the monthly sales report I asked you about a few months ago?
Manager	Oh yes! I told you then that I didn't want my name removed from the circulation list; it has got some interesting stuff in it.
Chief Executive	Has there been anything that's been particularly useful in the past few months?
Manager	I can't recall off the top of my head but I probably found something relevant at the time.
Chief Executive	I'm not surprised you can't recall anything. I had your name removed from the circulation list along with all the departmental managers three months ago. Only two out of eight people noticed they were no longer receiving the report. It just shows how much attention people paid to it. Your name has been permanently removed from the circulation list – if anything particularly relevant to your department is happening in future I've asked Sales to let you know.

Myth: 'But people ignore you unless it's in writing!'

Reality: People find it just as easy to ignore you when you put it in writing!

If you wandered round your office, you would find dozens of letters and memos, requesting urgent action, hibernating at the bottom of people's in-trays. In fact most people adopt the approach: 'I'll leave it there and if nobody rings me about it then I know it's not important.' You can bombard your colleagues with as many memos as you like but the best way to get them to do something is to go and ask them nicely. This approach is well illustrated by the scenario below:

Sue   Hi Geoff, I'm just ringing to see if you've pulled the figures together for me yet. Remember I sent you a memo about it two weeks ago!

Geoff   Oh yes! I have it here on the desk, I'll get on to it straight away. (Now where did I put that memo? I think it's under this pile here . . .)

If you want something done – put it in writing and mark it urgent!

The bureaucrat will argue that even if the job hasn't been done at least you will have the written proof that you asked for something to be done. Therefore you can't get the blame. But what about the following scenario?

Chief Executive   Sue, where are the figures? You were supposed to have them ready for this meeting.

Sue   Well, I sent Geoff a memo weeks ago asking for the information but he has done nothing about it!

Geoff   What memo? Are you sure you sent it?

Sue   I distinctly remember putting it in your in-tray myself.

Geoff   Well, I haven't seen it!

Myth: 'But if I don't write it down people won't know what to do!'

Reality: People are more productive if they are allowed to use their common sense.

Bureaucrats just love producing memos and instructions telling people what to do. They find nothing more satisfying than pointing out that the written procedures must be followed or pulling out the manual to prove that someone has done something wrong. Most manuals are ignored by the people they are aimed at – there's other work to be done!

Admin Manager   Here's our new manual, we've spent ages working on it. It should tell people exactly what to do in any given situation

– no matter how obscure. We've covered every possible contingency and every possible eventuality. It's a wealth of information – just listen to that resounding thud as it hits the desk, it's worth its weight in gold.

Salesperson We used to get along just fine until they created that new department at head office. It started off with them sending us instructions on how to do the job. Most of it went straight in the bin – it was just stuff telling us what we already knew. Next they started to introduce all these forms and checklists to go along with the instructions to make sure we carried them out. Next we get this 300-page manual which pulls together all those thing we used to throw in the bin. Those bureaucrats at head office haven't got a clue what it's like here at the front line. They think that if we have a problem we can sit down, put our feet up and browse through the manual to find out what to do. We're under pressure here so if a customer has a problem, you've got to use your common sense to sort it out and if you don't know what to do, you ask somebody. I guarantee you that the only time those manuals will be used is to prove someone did something wrong.

Myth: 'But others need to know what's happening in my department!'

Reality: Others are too busy with their own problems to worry about what you're up to!

'Marketing news — read all about us!'

As office workers we are guilty of seeing ourselves and our departments as being at the centre of the organization. As a result memos, newsletters and reports are mass circulated to keep everyone abreast of new developments and ongoing activities in our department. When others send us this 'for your information' and 'what's going on' paperwork it is usually pushed aside, unread, because we're too busy with other things. Yet we never stop to consider that our colleagues might find our 'self-promotion' paperwork irrelevant. Could the following conversation take place beside a photocopier near you?

Manager	Have you seen the latest report from Marketing?
Colleague	Yes, my desk is groaning under the weight of it. That's Fred for you – out to impress the Chief Executive again.
Manager	Have you read it yet?
Colleague	You're joking! I have a hundred and one other things on my desk which are more important. It's all very interesting, I'm sure but I don't have time to read about their new appointments, their staff party or how the company would fall apart if they weren't doing such a good job. There are too many people around here who suffer from the 'look at me' syndrome. I could send out reports like that every month but I'm too busy – it must have taken a week to put together and photocopy!

Myth: 'But I'd lose control if I got rid of it!'

Reality: Paperwork only creates the illusion of being in control.

I often encounter a fear in organizations that reducing paperwork will lower business standards. Managers recoil with shock at the thought of the chaos that would ensue if their precious procedures and control systems were scrapped.

Those organizations that have taken the minimal paper route find not surprisingly that the predicted chaos doesn't materialize but in fact productivity and morale increases. Tight control systems which demand that everything is documented only serve to shift attention away from the 'real work'. People waste their time filling in paperwork instead of concentrating on the job they are being paid to do. Furthermore, as the following scenario illustrates, those bureaucratic managers who rely excessively on paperwork to control their staff rarely have a clear idea of what is going on.

Dept Head   Nothing happens in this department without my knowledge – I check up on all incoming and outgoing correspondence. I also have a comprehensive reporting system in place which involves this pile of reports and forms here. And of course there's the procedures manual – I run a tight ship here without ever having to leave my office.

Subordinate   We tell him what he wants to hear – it makes life easier for us! He's a control freak and that means we have to fill in mountains of forms – but just because someone has filled in a bit of paper it doesn't mean the job was done, that it was done well or even that the right job was being done in the first place. We all dread the day when he leaves his office and finds out what's really going on. It's a lot easier to gloss over the truth in a report than when somebody is standing right in front of you asking you what's going on.

Myth: 'It's only one bit of paper, it can't do any harm!'

Reality: Paper creates work creates paper!

This is one of the most dangerous bureaucratic myths. If no other excuse can be thought of to justify a document it is held up as the source says 'It's only one bit of paper, what harm can it possibly do?' Unfortunately it can do a lot of harm because in the bureaucratic organization documents rarely exist in isolation – they tend to give rise to a chain of related work and paper. A new form created by one department may give rise to another form elsewhere in the organization or to a new monthly report which analyses the information collected. A single memo can set off a complex chain of replies and responses between dozens of people. If the information is important and carefully targeted then everyone in the chain can add value to it but when a dead, fat, dump or junk document is circulated a trail of wasted time and effort is created. In the following scenario a single memo swiftly creates a mountain of related paperwork.

Sales Manager	Hi, Liz, I'm glad I bumped into you. Did you get the memo I sent you?
Personnel Manager	Yes, I did. Thanks for keeping me in the loop. I thought Mike and Peter should be informed so I sent them copies along with the relevant pages from our current

policy manual. Peter e-mailed me querying whether or not the policy applies to his staff. I've sent you a copy of his memo and the reply. I also copied in the other departmental managers and the Chief Executive. I've had a number of replies and people seem to be a bit confused about what's going on so I've decided to set up a meeting to discuss the issues. I'll send you a draft agenda so you can make any necessary changes before I send it to the others.

Sales Manager Oh fine!

Exploding these bureaucratic myths is an essential part of the journey to conquer the information mountain. Before you can successfully challenge others to change their behaviour you will need to break out of your own 'put it in writing!' mind-set by identifying and overcoming your own bureaucratic myths.

CHAPTER THREE

Preparing for the Assault

'It's the nature of the business — there's nothing we can do about it!'

In this chapter we will look at the preparations that are necessary before a full-scale war on paperwork can be launched within the organization. Initially, to quantify how much paperwork is being circulated around the organization, and how much information you have on file, a paperwork audit will need to be conducted. Once you have gauged how bad things really are you will need to construct a plan that will serve as a road map in your journey towards the minimal paper office. Finally, with your plan complete, you will need to assemble a powerful team of bureaucracy-bashers to implement it.

In my experience 95 per cent of all paperwork reduction initiatives fail and this figure should be borne in mind when you are tempted to rush through the three preparation phases of the campaign. If you and your colleagues are prepared to attack the information mountain with passion and are determined to do whatever it takes to change the culture of the organization, you will have a fighting chance of overcoming the forces resisting change. However, if your campaign is launched by someone with little credibility, who is also busy with other things, your information mountain will continue to grow.

CONDUCT A PAPERWORK AUDIT
(WEEKS 1–6)

The paperwork audit involves finding out just how much paperwork and information is circulated and stored throughout the organization on an annual basis. If you don't have this information before you start the campaign you cannot set realistic paperwork reduction targets and you will have no way of knowing whether things have got better or worse as a result of your efforts. Beware of relying on rough estimates to measure the size of your information mountain – you will always fall way short of the actual figure. A senior manager of one financial institution argued that there was no need to conduct an audit as he had already calculated the figures 'on the back of an envelope'. His estimates were as follows – with the actual figures in brackets: 20 forms (86); 48 separate reports generated annually (435); 1 million computer printouts (13 million); 8 tonnes of files (156). After completing paperwork audits most organizations find that the volume of circulating paperwork and information is about 20 times greater than initial estimates.

Your audit also needs to be more comprehensive than a glance at the photocopier counter or a call to the office manager to find out how many reams of paper were purchased last year. In a process that will take several weeks you will need to tour the organization to find out what reports, forms, correspondence, manuals and other types of paperwork are: (a) received by each department, (b) sent out by each department and (c) circulated within each department. The audit should also involve estimating the volume and types of document that are stored in filing cabinets and on the shelves of each department. Often omitted from paperwork audits is an examination of the flow and storage of electronic documents. While this is a slightly more difficult exercise because virtual paper is invisible, failure to complete it will perpetuate the myth in the organization that all electronic information is good and that all paper is bad. Ultimately all your junk will end up on computer!

As well as calculating the size of your information mountain your audit should also estimate the annual costs of generating, circulating and storing it. You will need to calculate your annual filing costs, mailing costs, printing costs, stationery costs and equipment costs.

The detailed statistics you obtain from the paperwork audit will help you to build support for the campaign at all levels in the organization. A vague plea along the lines of 'We're buried under a mountain of paperwork and we need to do something about it!' will do little to motivate your colleagues to act. Standing up at your next management meeting, however, and making a statement similar to the following will get people's attention! 'We currently circulate 8 million sheets of paper and 12 million sheets of electronic information – an annual paper trail of 3,800 miles. We aim to reduce both figures by 25 per cent. We also hoard 30 million sheets of paper weighing 160 tonnes, with another 42 million sheets on disk and our aim is to reduce both those figures by 50 per cent. If we achieve these targets our operating costs will be cut by £1.5 million per annum.' Your opinion that things need to change needs to be supported by fact because not everyone will agree with you.

As well as finding out the hard facts the paperwork audit

is an opportunity to collect anecdotal evidence about the harmful effects of bureaucratic paperwork. People will be only too happy to entertain you with horror stories of fat reports, complex forms, incomprehensible manuals and verbose memos – generated by other departments of course! You should also ask people to justify the paperwork they generate and circulate to others. You will build up a long list of the bureaucratic myths that are used throughout the organization and this will give you the chance to start preparing your arguments against them. If in conducting the audit you come across paperwork that is universally detested, try to eliminate it immediately as early successes will help to win support for the campaign.

'Tut, tut! Fred. I'm afraid you're going to have to go on a strict paperwork diet.'

How high is your reports mountain?

Identify all the reports that each department churns out on a routine basis and obtain copies of their circulation lists. Then calculate the annual volume of soft- or hard-copy paperwork generated by each report and produce a Top 10 list of the fattest reports in the organization. Ask the author of each report why it is generated – you will be surprised at the number of people that won't be able to give you an immediate answer! Find out how much time is spent handling each report by asking its creator how long it takes to put the report together, and then at the other end of the paper trail finding out how long recipients spend reading it – if at all! Ad hoc reports should not be left out of your audit as they are just as prevalent and more likely to fall under the heading of non-essential paperwork. Ask a representative sample of people how many ad hoc reports they have generated in the past twelve months and produce an estimate of the total number circulating annually.

How high is your memo mountain?

If you are still circulating memos on paper, you shouldn't feel at a disadvantage compared with e-mail users in other organizations. The flow of irrelevant paper memos is but a trickle compared with the torrent of information generated by e-mail. To estimate the number of memos produced annually within the organization ask a representative sample of staff to list all the paper and e-mail memos they send and receive in one month. Find out from your sample group what proportion of the memos they receive fall into the categories of dead, fat, dump and junk paperwork. Calculate how much time people spend reading and responding to memos in a typical week. Produce a league table of departments according to the number of memos they generate and try to shame people into taking talk more seriously.

How high is your standard forms mountain?

Uncovering all the different forms used in your organization is a more difficult task than it at first appears. In conducting a paperwork audit for a large pharmaceutical company I asked one department head how many forms were used in his department. 'One or two, we're not really a form-heavy organization' was the reply. Within two hours, however, I had uncovered 17 different forms which generated over 50,000 pieces of paper a year! As you identify each form follow it through its life-cycle to find out how many people handle it and what supplementary paperwork it spawns. Ask the people who have to fill in the form to comment on its usefulness. Could the job be done without the form? Could it be simplified? Could it be merged with another form? At the end of the paper trail check to ensure that the information requested by the form is actually used. Find out who retains copies of the form on file and why. Produce a Top 10 list of all the forms used in the organization ranked according to the volume of paperwork they generate and the number of people who handle them. Don't forget to include all those forms that have been computerized – just because they have disappeared into the computer does not mean that all the work associated with them has been eliminated.

How high is your manuals mountain?

Scour the shelves of the organization and look deep in departmental filing cabinets to identify all the policy and procedure manuals that are currently in print. Don't be afraid to take away a copy of each manual – nobody will notice they're gone! Talk to those who produce each manual and find out how much time and effort goes into producing it and how much paperwork is generated in the process. Ask them what purpose the manual serves and how often they expect it to be used. Then talk to the target audience for the manual and find out how useful they consider it to be and how often they refer to it.

How high is your correspondence mountain?

A trip to the postroom to get the figures on incoming and outgoing correspondence will leave you stunned. The direct mail industry is flourishing and there will be a constant flow of leaflets, brochures and information packs both in and out of your organization. In addition there is the normal business correspondence between you and your suppliers and customers. Identify the main sources of information from outside the organization and calculate how much information is generated by each one. Question the recipients about the value of incoming information and how much time they spend processing it. Then look at your outgoing correspondence and identify the main destinations for paperwork generated within the organization.

How high is your photocopy mountain?

Your office manager should be able to tell you exactly how much paper is consumed by the organization's photocopiers on an annual basis. If you have recently installed an electronic mail network, find out if the volume of photocopies has dropped dramatically as a result — don't be surprised if it has increased. Produce a breakdown of photocopies by department and focus on the photocopy hotspots by asking questions like: Why do you generate so many copies? Is your photocopy mountain made up of occasional bulk runs or frequent small runs? Could you survive if we removed your photocopier?

How high is your computer printout mountain?

The paperless office proponents often overlook the fact that every computer is linked up to a printer which constantly churns out memos, reports, correspondence, e-mail messages and other documents. Obtain the printout statistics from your office manager or your IT colleagues and produce a departmental league table highlighting the worst offenders.

How high is your files and records mountain?

In calculating the size of your files and records mountain you should start with the documents hoarded in the organization's filing cabinets — a standard file drawer will hold about 4,000 pieces of paper. Your attention should then turn to the documents that are filed on disk. Take a representative staff sample and calculate the number of documents they have filed electronically on their desktop PCs and what the paper equivalent is. One megabyte of memory on your PC is roughly equivalent to 4,000 pages of text. Don't forget to include corporate archives that are stored centrally or off-site. As well as finding out the total volume of information currently held on file try to estimate the growth in electronic and paper files. Rank departments according to the volume of information they hoard on file.

When your audit has been completed you should end up with a set of figures similar to the ones in the box below. From the figures you have collected calculate the height, weight and length of your annual paperwork output.

HOW MUCH PAPER CAN 100 BUREAUCRATS GENERATE IN A YEAR?

8 tonnes – 625 feet – 284 miles

The following figures were compiled from paperwork audits in 11 organizations, all with over 200 office staff. It was found that on average 100 office workers will handle 1,500,000 pieces of hard- and soft-copy paperwork annually, a paper mountain equivalent to 8 tonnes. The quantities of each different category of paperwork handled are listed below:

Reports	95,000
Memos	238,000
Outgoing correspondence	387,000
Incoming correspondence	256,000
Photocopies	1,200,000
Computer printouts	1,086,000
Standard forms	11,000

Manuals	77,000
Printed material	1,320,000
The total volume of information held on file per 100 office staff:	
Paper files	4,000,000
Electronic files	17,000,000

How high is your paper mountain?

After conducting your paperwork audit you will have a set of figures similar to those above and from them you should calculate the height, weight and length of your paper output. Based on the research above and assuming that 100 A4 sheets of paper are approximately half an inch thick, organizations produce an annual paper mountain of 6625 feet for every 100 office workers. Each individual handles a stack of papers 6.25 feet high per annum. Of course there is a wide variance here with some people handling only a small amount of paper while others grapple annually with stacks of paper which are 30–40 feet high.

How heavy is your paper mountain?

One hundred A4 sheets of paper weigh approximately 1.2 lbs. Therefore for every 100 office workers organizations produce a stack of paper annually that weighs more than 8 tonnes. In addition the equivalent of 112 tonnes of paper are held on file.

How long is your paper trail?

With A4 paper being approximately one foot long, 100 office workers generate an annual paper trail of 284 miles. Laid end to end their files would stretch for nearly 4,000 miles.

CONSTRUCT A PAPERWORK REDUCTION PLAN (WEEKS 7–10)

Having conducted the paperwork audit you will have built up a good picture of just how heavily you and your colleagues rely on paper. The next step in your bid to conquer the paper mountain is to construct a plan that will guide you in the transition from an information-heavy bureaucracy to a minimal paper office. Unfortunately many well-meaning managers rush headlong at the paper mountain shouting and screaming about the problem. Without a clear vision of where they want to end up in the long term, however, they are easily deflected by short-term failures. Without any thought of the paradox involved memos are mass circulated demanding that less paperwork be generated, newsletter articles tell people about the problems of excess paperwork and voluminous reports are written on the paperwork problem. One local government records manager produced a 40-page booklet for each one of the 3,000 staff with a 'think before you print' theme. If only they had followed their own advice! – 120,000 extra pieces of paper cluttered up the organization's desks, filing cabinets and shelves while there was no noticeable decrease in circulating paperwork as a result of the booklet. If you've already tried such fluffy, quick-fix solutions in the past you

will have experienced similar results – nothing changes!
Taking the time to produce a well-thought-out, credible

'He always goes for the 'quick-fix' solution – says he's too busy to plan.'

plan will help you to build support and momentum for the
campaign throughout the organization – especially from
senior management without whose support your campaign
will never get off the ground. The planning process will also
help you to prepare and rehearse your arguments for dealing with the inevitable resistance from those trying to block
the campaign. You should expect to be bombarded with an
avalanche of excuses such as the ones below that have all
been used to successfully smother ill-prepared paperwork
reduction proposals in other organizations.

IT WON'T WORK BECAUSE . . .

- 'It's the nature of the business we're in'
- 'Yes, there is a lot of paper but we seem to get by!'
- 'Things will just go back to normal in a few months!'
- 'You can't stop people generating unnecessary paper-work!'
- 'We've already tried that a few years ago – it didn't work!'
- 'I think we need more paperwork around here not less!'
- 'We're too busy with other things at the moment!'
- 'We're not as bad as some other organizations'

Laying out a detailed plan will also help you to overcome the dangerous tendency to commit insufficient time and resources to the campaign. As you will see later in this chapter the minimal paper office can only be achieved by releasing, full-time, people with the necessary authority and credibility to push through the proposed changes.

The first output from your planning process should be a one-page project proposal similar to the example below. This should be presented to the chief executive and other senior managers who are likely to support the campaign. Once you have secured senior management support and assembled your campaign team you should take them away from the office for several days to construct a more detailed project plan. Each of the nine stages in the minimal paper office project should be broken down into a series of tasks which should then be allocated to a member of the project team – project manager, team members, chief executive, consultant, departmental champions or support staff. The duration of each task should then be estimated and a project schedule produced. A clear plan will remove much of the uncertainty that always accompanies the change from a 'put it in writing' culture to a minimal paper one. Once people can see the different stages of the plan in black and white it prepares them for the changes that lie ahead and removes some of the uncertainty. A paperwork reduction campaign without a plan will go nowhere.

MINIMAL PAPER OFFICE PROJECT PROPOSAL

PROJECT OUTLINE

The minimal paper office project will streamline the organization's information and paperwork by identifying and eliminating everything that is non-essential. The project will also achieve a culture shift in the organization from the current 'put it in writing' approach to a 'minimal paper' one.

BACKGROUND INFORMATION

A paperwork audit was conducted in June to find out how much paperwork was circulating throughout the organization on an annual basis. It was discovered that 33,000 miles of paper pass across people's desks every year and the organization has 80 tonnes of paper on file with the equivalent of 200 tonnes of paper stored on disk. When questioned, people said that approximately 30–40 per cent of the internal paperwork that arrived on their desks was unnecessary. The annual cost of generating, distributing and storing all this paperwork is estimated to be greater than £2 million. Furthermore people are complaining that they can't do the jobs they are being paid to do because their attention is deflected by all this bureaucratic paperwork. We have invested considerable amounts of time and money in our pursuit of the paperless office but technology has created vast amounts of virtual paperwork without really reducing the volume of hard-copy paper.

OBJECTIVES
1 To reduce circulating information and paperwork by 25 per cent over the next 12 months
2 To reduce electronic and paper files by 50 per cent
3 To train all staff to think and act in a 'minimal paper' way

PROJECT STAGES
1 Conduct paperwork audit (weeks 1–6)
2 Assemble a paperwork reduction team (weeks 7–10)
3 Construct a minimal paper office plan (weeks 11–14)
4 Launch the campaign (weeks 15–18)
5 Create a paperwork reduction exhibition (weeks 19–25)
6 Hold Conquer the Information Mountain! workshops for all staff (weeks 26–36)
7 Organize a Clear Your Desk! day (weeks 37–39)
8 Conduct a paperchase (weeks 40–51)
9 Review the project (week 52)

KEY PLAYERS

It is anticipated that a full-time team of three people will be required for a period of 12 months. The project manager should be a senior manager who has the credibility to push through the necessary changes. The remaining members of the team should be front-line staff rather than support people. The chief executive should launch the campaign, spend time checking on its progress and demonstrate his support by occasionally tearing up junk paperwork. It is also proposed to use a consultant who has experience with such campaigns to speed up the process and maximize our chances of success. Support staff will need to be released at various stages during the project.

COSTS

The total costs for the campaign will be £55,000 which includes setting up the exhibition, consultancy and training.

BENEFITS

As a result of the campaign the organization will:
- Reduce annual operating costs by £2,000,000
- Increase revenue by 5 per cent
- Avoid capital investment costs of £300,000
- Free up 50,000 hours of staff time previously spent on administration
- Improve morale with the removal of bureaucratic paperwork

ASSEMBLE YOUR PAPERWORK REDUCTION TEAM (WEEKS 11–14)

You have now reached the most important step of the project – putting together a team with the skills and determination necessary to conquer the information mountain. The quality of your team members and the amount of time they devote to the project will ultimately determine how successful it is.

The paperwork reduction team

The members of your project team should be encamped in a special project 'war room' which will increase the visibility of the project and also serve as a model 'minimal paper' environment. Taking team members away from their desks will build team spirit, cut down on distractions and reduce the conflict of interest between their normal duties and their project duties. It may seem an obvious point but your campaign team should generate only the minimum amount of paperwork necessary to make the campaign a success. Under no circumstances should they have access to a photocopier and any member of the team generating more than

10 documents in a week should be removed immediately! During the course of one consulting assignment I visited the project team after being away for a week. In that time they had invented three new forms, circulated an update report to all department heads, sent over 300 e-mail messages and were in the process of putting together a paperwork reduction manual. The roles and responsibilities of the key players in your minimal paper office project are outlined below.

Chief executive

Senior executives are usually only too ready to back the campaign as they suffer more than most at the hands of the bureaucrats within the organization. The chief executive of a major airline recounts the following story:

> I came back from a trip away and there was a two-foot pile of papers in my in-tray and about ninety e-mail messages on my computer. I separated all the documents into three different categories. First, there was the 'look at me paperwork' from people wanting to let me know what a great job they were doing. Secondly, there was the 'cover your ass' paperwork from people telling me that something could go wrong but it wasn't their fault, and finally there was the paperwork that required action. Of that pile everything had been dealt with in my absence except for three items. I told my PA that in future these are the only three things I want landing on my desk.

Of course people throughout the organization are aware of

the need for change and many minimal paper campaigns are initiated at middle management levels. If the campaign is to be a success, the chief executive must become involved at some stage. The chief executive's authority is required to release people from their normal duties to join the project team and to reassure staff that no jobs will be lost as a result of the campaign. Chief executives should also support the campaign by their actions – taking their names off circulation lists, refusing to read fat reports, tearing up bureaucratic forms, pulling people up for generating paperwork instead of talking to each other. The chief executive's diary should also reflect his interest in the campaign – dropping in on the project team at least once a week, visiting departments to review their progress, attending the paperwork reduction exhibition and seminars. Resistance to the campaign will be surprisingly limited if the chief executive is visiting different departments and asking people what paperwork they have personally eliminated since the launch of the campaign. The chief executive should also make a point of recognizing and rewarding those who have eliminated bad paperwork and embraced the minimal paper approach.

Project manager

While the chief executive should be seen as the visionary behind the campaign the project manager is the person responsible for ensuring that the everything moves forward on a day-to-day basis. Your project manager should be a charismatic 'fast-track' person with a proven history of success in managing other high-level projects. Unless you have to fight tooth and nail to get them released from their normal duties they are probably not worth having. They should be senior enough to be able to walk into any department, scrutinize its operations and then insist that certain paperwork is simplified or eliminated if necessary. Your project manager should ideally be a front-line person, someone who has had first-hand experience at grappling with a mountain of distracting paperwork. They will be straining at the leash to do some bureaucracy-bashing unlike a support person whose own paperwork is likely to be the target of the campaign.

Your project manager should already have a reputation within his or her own department for detesting bureaucracy and paperwork. There may be stories of forms being torn up, of a refusal to read any report longer than two pages or of memos being banned. If you don't have someone in-house with the determination to change things you will need to hire in someone who has conducted a successful streamlining exercise elsewhere.

Core team members

The core members of the project team should also be front-line people who are frustrated about the volume of paperwork passing across their desks and who are highly motivated to scrap what is non-essential. There should be a feeling amongst team members that 'the sooner we sort this mess out the sooner we can get back to work'. They should have a good knowledge of different areas of the business so that they are not easily deflected by bureaucratic myth smokescreens. There is always the danger of team members concentrating on the junk paperwork generated by others while ignoring their own. Therefore the first task for the team should be to look at ways of reducing the paperwork they generate as part of their normal jobs, and ways of keeping project paperwork to an absolute minimum. Once they have learned to help themselves they are in a much better position to help others.

Under no circumstances should support staff be allowed to hijack the campaign – they should be used only on an ad hoc basis to complement the skills of the core team members. Administration staff may help in conducting the paperwork audits and paperchase; IT people can help in identifying and eliminating non-essential electronic information; legal people can be seconded when the team is looking at setting up a retention schedule for files in the organization and financial staff will prove useful in calculating the cost savings resulting from the campaign.

The size of the organization and the scale of the information mountain will obviously dictate the size of your project team and the amount of time they are released for. A rule of thumb that I use for determining the amount of time that should be devoted to a project is 'one day for every person in the organisation'. Thus a staff of 100 would require one person working for 20 weeks on the project and a staff of 1,000 would require a team of four, working for a year on the project. The members of the project team should be released from their normal duties for two or three days a week, if not full-time.

Departmental champions

A paperwork reduction champion should be sought out in

each department to assist the campaign team during the project. These champions should be among the first to change their own behaviour and to break out of their bureaucratic mind-set. They can then be used as role models for their colleagues. During the paperwork audit they can collect information on the reports, forms and other types of paperwork passing across their colleagues' desks. They can also assist in implementing paperwork reduction proposals and give regular feedback to members of the project team on the progress of the campaign. Where there is a desire to reduce an inter-departmental information flow they can sit down with colleagues from that department to look at ways of simplifying things.

Consultant

Consultants, while they should never be allowed to take ownership of the project away from their own staff, can provide invaluable assistance throughout the campaign. They bring with them important lessons learned from mistakes made by other organizations and this experience will greatly increase your chances of success. The old adage that it is impossible to become a 'guru' within your own company holds true and consultants often serve as the catalysts that get the minimal paper office project off the ground. Managers who have previously ignored pleas from their own colleagues to reduce paperwork will often respond enthusiastically to the same message coming from an external source. The independent status of the consultant means they have not been indoctrinated into the organization's bureaucratic mind-set and can more clearly see through the bureaucratic myths that are used to justify unnecessary paperwork.

During the planning phase the consultant can help you to anticipate and avoid the bureaucratic roadblocks that lie ahead and your plan is more likely to succeed when faced with the real world. During staff training the consultant's stories of successful bureaucracy-bashing elsewhere can inspire those who were previously apathetic about change.

The danger with consultants is that they tend to produce 'telephone book' reports suggesting widespread changes but then do little to help in the implementation of those rec-ommendations. When choosing a consultant you should therefore look for an 'action not paperwork' mentality. If a prospective consultant sends you an initial proposal which is more than five pages long – you are probably talking to the wrong person!

The preparation phase of your minimal paper office pro-ject will have taken approximately three months and if you have followed all the advice in this chapter you can now launch the project with confidence. If for reasons of laziness, insufficient passion or lack of senior management support your preparation is inadequate then your campaign will be over before you know it. The blockers will take hold of your arguments and rip them to shreds leaving you no closer to the minimal paper office.

CHAPTER FOUR

Attacking the Information Mountain

'They want me to reduce my files by 80 per cent without hiding them in the computer! Where do I start?!'

In this chapter we'll look at what happens between weeks 15–39 of your campaign. From launching the campaign, setting up a paperwork reduction exhibition, running Conquer the Information Mountain! workshops for all staff to organizing a Clear Your Desk! day. The aim of these four project stages is to build support and momentum for the campaign throughout the organization. The initial push for change must come from the top down but if the campaign is to be successful in the long term you will have to win the hearts and minds of staff at all levels.

LAUNCH THE CAMPAIGN (WEEKS 15–18)

The war against bad paperwork must be launched by your chief executive – a plea to change from lower down the organization lacks credibility and authority and will consequently be ignored. People will be too busy dealing with the issues the chief executive is openly concerned about.

The one-page dictate below was pinned to notice-boards throughout a large service business. The chief executive had earlier launched the campaign at the company conference by standing on stage and tearing into shreds more than 50 documents that had recently arrived on his desk from 'paper shuffling' colleagues. He also read out a selection of the 60 junk e-mail messages he had received during the previous month. To accompany his tirade against excess paperwork he showed a video he had made the night before after everyone had gone home. He had toured the organization's offices with his camcorder to record the chaotic mountains of paperwork hibernating on people's desks and in their filing systems.

To: All staff
Re: THE MINIMAL PAPER OFFICE CAMPAIGN

Last year we generated an astonishing 20 million photocopies, 17 million computer printouts and 2 million standard forms. I would estimate that 40 per cent of that paperwork was completely unnecessary. It seems that our energies are becoming increasingly directed towards paper pushing rather than on work that is of value to the company. In a bid to reverse this unacceptable trend the MINIMAL PAPER OFFICE CAMPAIGN has been launched. The campaign will identify and eliminate all non-essential paperwork in the organization – both hard- and soft-copy. A paperwork reduction target of 25 per cent has been set for the next 12 months.

This is not a campaign to save trees, it is a campaign to prevent our most important resource – people – from suffocating under a mountain of bureaucratic paperwork. Nobody has a divine right to bombard their colleagues with paper or to constantly demand information from them. Everyone I talk to in the organization agrees with that sentiment but blames 'others' for the problem. This campaign will be a resounding success if just one person changes – YOU! From today you should adopt the following minimal paper principles:

Justify it or scrap it!	Continually question the value of all paperwork and eliminate anything that is unnecessary.
KISS!	(Keep it simple, stupid!) Find the easiest way to do the job well.
GOYA!	(Get off your ass!) If you want to collect or disseminate information go and talk to people. Only put it in writing as a last resort.
Take talk seriously!	Verbal communication should carry the same weight as written communication.
Action not paperwork	Try to solve problems rather than writing about them.
Hands off!	Don't handle paperwork that could be deal with by others.
AOR!	(Available on request!) Don't circulate information indiscriminately. Tell people where they can find it if they need it.
One in – one out!	Only introduce new paperwork if you can eliminate something that is obsolete.

Speak out! Always give immediate feedback to those who send you unnecessary information.

Be brief! Don't burden your colleagues with excess information.

This document has been produced in accordance with my new 'one page' policy – please show the same consideration when writing to me.

The chief executive's message was backed up by a full-blown internal communications campaign. An article in the company's newsletter focused on the need for change by highlighting some internal bureaucratic horror stories. In one week the divisional sales managers had received eight forms from head office all of which requested information that had previously been provided or that was readily available from computer records. Early success stories were also highlighted. The marketing department had decided to scrap its customer survey forms and do something that had not been considered in the past – talk to customers. The information collected by direct communication was of a much higher quality and a new product line was to be launched as a result. A special paperwork reduction telephone number was launched which allowed people to leave their ideas anonymously on an answering machine – an initiative that led to more than 200 responses. Posters were created which illustrated the 'Be brief' theme and ten guidelines were given on how to avoid long-winded documents. Those producing the organization's video newsletter visited a company of similar size that had already success-fully conquered the information mountain. All the managers interviewed emphasized the ruthless approach that was necessary to break down the bureaucratic barriers to change.

In consulting for organizations I am frequently asked for advice on the tone the campaign should take. Some will opt for a persuasive, cajoling approach while others will argue that the changes need to be bulldozed through. With any major change there initially tends to be a 'wait around and let's see what happens' approach. People will have seen too many past initiatives launched with great fervour but then forgotten about as soon as something else came along. Once your colleagues see that you have the commitment to see the changes through they will enthusiastically support the campaign. There will of course be resistors (that 10 per cent of people who are against everything all of the time!) and while they should be persuaded of the wisdom of the pro-posed changes they should also be reminded that the changes will be bulldozed through regardless of whether they are in the way or not.

If the chief executive is involved you can expect circulat-ing paperwork to be cut by about 10 per cent during the first six weeks of the campaign. This will mainly be due to people holding back on one-off memos and other docu-ments, or reducing their circulation lists. The company's photocopiers, printers and e-mail networks will certainly be quieter but no fundamental changes will yet have taken place. Things will return to normal in a few months if, com-placent with your initial success, you fail to move on to the next stage of the campaign. And remember, the fear factor can only work for as long as the chief executive is on the warpath.

ORGANIZE A PAPERWORK REDUCTION EXHIBITION (WEEKS 19–25)

The next stage in your journey towards the minimal paper office is to set up a paperwork reduction exhibition which will illustrate both the scale of the organization's current problems and the desired future state – the minimal paper office.

Much of the information you collected during the paperwork audit can now be put to good use. A central display should be created to show the total volume of paperwork circulating around the organization on an annual basis. One government department calculated that it generated an annual stack of paper 45 times higher than its 20-storey office block while a manufacturing organization calculated that the weight of the paper it circulated was actually greater than the weight of all the products it produced. Separate displays should also be created for the different types of paperwork circulating around the organization – standard forms, photocopies, correspondence, reports, memos, manuals, faxes, files, customer paperwork, supplier paperwork. The display for each type of paperwork should show the volume generated annually along with its costs and the number of hours spent handling it. A display should also be used to highlight the volume of electronic paper generated annually by the organization. This display should emphasize the fact that hiding paperwork in the computer is *not* the solution to the paper problem.

'No, it isn't the exhibition — it's just Mike producing a new manual.'

The standand forms display would for example contain an example of each form used in the organization. A Top 10 list of forms should show the quantity of paper generated by each form along with the number of manhours needed to process it and its annual costs. The display might also contain some anecdotal evidence of the problems caused by bad forms — customers finding the forms too complex, forms asking for information that could be obtained more quickly and inexpensively elsewhere. One utility company discovered that 23 separate forms had to be filled in between a customer complaint and repair of the fault. This horrendous paper trail was illustrated by photographs of people handling the paperwork at each stage of the process — the display took up the whole of 10×30 foot wall. It was clear to everyone looking at the display that many stages in the paper trail were unnecessary and within three months 21 of the forms had been scrapped. Your display should also have some of the statistics compiled during the paperwork audit along the lines of those below.

- Standard forms account for 15 per cent of the paperwork we generate on an annual basis
- We have 47 separate forms generating 3 million sheets of paper per annum
- Laid end to end our forms would create a paper trail of 568 miles
- Our annual printing costs for forms is £62,000
- The cost of photocopying forms is £42,000 annually
- We spend 450,000 hours handling electronic and paper forms annually
- The total cost of printing and processing forms is £1,500,000 per annum

A forms reduction target of between 20–80 per cent should also be highlighted.

All the organization's staff should be given a guided tour of the exhibition and without exception they will be amazed at the sheer volume of paperwork and information that the company generates on an annual basis. As people walk from display to display you will hear comments such as 'I can't believe we generate so much paperwork to run what should be a relatively simple business. The time we waste on paper processing could go into *real* work.'

The exhibition should be not used as a forum for blaming individuals or focusing the spotlight on specific departments. Its purpose is to unite people behind a common cause not to castigate people for their past sins. If people feel threatened as they walk around the exhibition, it will increase their resistance to the campaign. If bad paperwork is highlighted, it should be something that is universally agreed to be unnecessary.

The second section of the exhibition should create a clear vision of the minimal paper office and how the organization can achieve it. The main stages of the minimal paper office project should be illustrated so that people can see exactly what changes will take place and what part they are expected to play in the process. A display should also be created to highlight the paperwork reduction principles (see Chapter Six) which will form the building blocks for the new minimal paper culture.

It is especially important that successes are highlighted during the early stages of the campaign. A special display should highlight paper reduction measures that have already been implemented. One organization created a display which listed each paperwork reduction measure and the volume of paper saved annually. A 'totalizer' updated on a weekly basis illustrated the total volume of paperwork saved as a result of the campaign to date. Success stories from other organizations should also be illustrated to encourage people to think about the changes they need to make.

While there will undoubtedly be many changes occurring as a result of the exhibition, people's habits are so ingrained that it only takes a few small problems for people to forget about the benefits of the minimal paper office and return to their old familiar ways. As one manager charged with banishing the bureaucratic culture recalls:

Our campaign was spectacularly successful in the first few months after the exhibition. People were genuinely shocked by what they saw and there was an almost universal desire to see things change. The volume of paperwork circulating around the office fell by more than 60 per cent. The chief executive was involved and people didn't want to engage his wrath so they were delaying certain memos and reports until the heat was off. People had a backlog of stuff they wanted to photocopy and distribute but were temporarily delaying it. I walked into one office and saw a huge pile of manuals stacked in the corner and, asking what they were, I was told that they were being held back until the campaign was over. Sure enough when the campaign had ended, and the chief executive's attention was deflected elsewhere, there was a huge damburst of paperwork. The paperholics who have been on an enforced paper diet reverted to their old habits and within six months the paper mountain was as bad as ever.

People need that extra push if the culture of the organization is to change in the long term. That push should come from the Conquer the Information Mountain! workshops.

HOLD CONQUER THE INFORMATION MOUNTAIN! WORKSHOPS (WEEKS 26–36)

Everyone who handles paper in the organization, from the chief executive down, should attend Conquer the Information Mountain! Workshops. These workshops take people out of the work environment and allow them to evaluate their paperwork generation and handling habits. They create awareness of the problems caused by the 'put it in writing' culture and fire people up with the enthusiasm necessary to rid the organization of excess paperwork.

Your bureaucratic colleagues will undoubtedly grumble about the time and expense involved in these workshops but the cost of not running them and remaining buried under a mountain of paperwork is many times greater. Don't compromise with the blockers by running workshops only for select groups of people – unless everyone in the organization attends, nobody will change. Some organizations will insist that only their senior managers attend and that the message can then be cascaded down the organization. Unfortunately the power of the message and the passion it generates tend to be diluted as it is passed from one person to another and the masses remain apathetic about the campaign. Being selective about who attends the workshops also creates the feeling among non-participants that excess paperwork is not their problem. The feeling tends to be 'If they had thought I could make a positive contribution to the campaign, they would have asked me to attend!'

The workshops should be led by an external consultant with the project manager and other members of the project team trained to act as facilitators. An external workshop leader can more easily challenge the status quo and ensure that the blockers do not take over the sessions and render them ineffective. Those opposing organizational change always seem to be more vocal than those supporting it. It is also worthwhile to invite someone from another organization to relate tales of their personal success stories in the war against paperwork. It is always tempting to use the in-house training department to run these workshops but nothing can be more injurious to the campaign. In-house sessions tend to be ineffective in dealing with resistance to change partly because those running the sessions lack credibility amongst senior management and partly because they are just as guilty of bureaucratic behaviour as those attending.

To give you a flavour of the right approach to take in the workshops some of the exercises I have found to be most useful are discussed below.

Who needs to change?

Workshop participants will always agree that things need to change if the minimal paper office is to be achieved. The disagreement always occurs when it comes down to who needs to change! Participants are given a blank A4 piece of paper along with a marker pen and are asked to think about the paperwork they handle – reports, memos, correspondence, forms, manuals and so on. They are then asked to write down the answer to the question: 'Who do you think most needs to change most for the paperwork reduction campaign to be a success?' People are told they can list individuals, departments or other groups of people inside or outside the organization. When everyone has written down their answer they are asked to simultaneously hold up their sheets of paper. People will nod at their colleagues who gave similar answers to their own: 'Yes, I have the same problems with those bureaucrats in marketing, administration, personnel, finance.' 'My boss is just as bad as yours' or 'My subordinates copy me in on everything as well.' There is of course only one right answer to the question 'Who needs to change most for the campaign to be a success?' – 'Myself.' The following illustration is then shown to illustrate the point:

There were four bureaucrats who worked together named Everybody, Somebody, Anybody and Nobody. They were all buried under a mountain of paperwork and were

delighted when it was decided that less junk should be circulated. Everybody was sure Somebody would do it. Anybody could have done it but Nobody did it. Somebody got angry about that because it was Everybody's job. Everybody thought Anybody could do it but Nobody realized that Everybody wouldn't do it. When the paperwork reduction campaign was a failure Everybody blamed Somebody because Nobody did what Anybody could have done.

Good v. Bad paperwork

Prior to the workshop participants are asked to collect examples of both the good and bad paperwork that arrives on their desks. During the workshop groups are asked to study these documents and to come up with defining principles for both good and bad paperwork. Back in the office when generating paperwork they will then be more likely to stop and ask themselves 'Is this good or bad?'

Paperwork reduction principles

The paperwork reduction principles outline the types of behaviour that are commonplace in the minimal paper office. It is not enough for people to be able to remember what the principles are; they must practise them religiously. After attending the workshops participants should have a clear idea about how each one of the paperwork reduction principles relates to their own work environment.

To get the 'speak out' message across participants might be asked to think of 10 ways of telling their colleagues to stop generating unnecessary paperwork – without offending them of course! For the 'hands off!' principle participants are given a case study which illustrates how a simple job is made complicated by too many people being involved in the process. They are asked to apply the principle to minimize the amount of work needed to get the job done. It can also be useful to split the group into pairs and ask each pair to prepare an internal marketing campaign to include posters, slogans, and rewards for one of the paperwork reduction principles.

Trimming the fat

As well as eliminating unnecessary paperwork the organization can make significant paper reductions by trimming the fat from important documents. After a discussion on the techniques of concise writing, a selection of memos, correspondence and other documents are handed out. One group of participants will be asked to rewrite the documents making them twice as long as the original without adding any useful information, while the second group is asked to edit the documents to half their size without removing any useful information. This exercise drives home the point that it is just as easy to be concise as it is to be long-winded.

Burying the dead

Bureaucrats don't like throwing anything away and they use a variety of excuses to justify their hoarding habit – the Top 10 are listed below. As well as taking up valuable space these dead files mean that the important information is often more difficult to find. A bulging filing cabinet is set up in the workshop room and as the flawed thinking behind each excuse is exposed, the documents hoarded using that excuse are discarded. By the time you have reached the tenth excuse the filing cabinet should only be about 20 per cent full.

Top 10 hoarding excuses
- If I leave the company, others will need it!
- My boss would hit the roof!
- Someone else might be interested!
- It may become relevant in the future!
- I'm going to look at it when I get the time!
- Others are bound to lose their copies!
- I don't want to offend the sender!
- There's no harm in keeping it!
- But it cost money!

Bureaucratic myths

Participants should also be encouraged to challenge their bureaucratic myths during the workshop. They should be asked to think of excuses to justify paperwork which everyone agrees is unnecessary. One real-life example I often use is of the manager from a large bank who received a copy of *Dentistry Today* every month. The speed with which participants can think of excuses to justify such paperwork will demonstrate how easy it is to slip into the bureaucratic mode.

Brainstorm 50 paperwork reduction ideas

Participants are asked to use the paperchase checklist in Chapter Five and to generate as many paperwork reduction ideas as they can in a five-minute period. The emphasis in the exercise is to suspend all critical judgement and no idea – however ridiculous – should be ignored. The idea for ATM machines came from a brainstorming session where some 'idiot' suggested that queues could be reduced by smashing a hole in the wall and allowing people to come in and help themselves to money. A properly faciliated and motivated group will come up with 50 or more paperwork reduction ideas. Once these ideas have been listed the group can work through them one by one to see how they can be implemented.

Back to the future

This exercise proves invaluable in helping participants to visualize the minimal paper office. It is also useful during the first stage of the campaign in formulating a plan and weighing up alternative courses of action. Participants are asked to envisage themselves two years into the future and told that a prominent business journalist has heard about the organization's successful war against paperwork. He has requested an interview with a member of the organization's staff to find out what has been happening. The participants are split into two groups with one group being asked to prepare a list of questions that the journalist might ask while the second is asked to prepare answers to possible questions. Each group elects one of their members to play the roles of interviewer and interviewee respectively. Some typical interview questions might be: Why did you think it necessary to launch this campaign? How has the organization benefited? Who was resistant to the campaign? How did you overcome resistance? What would you do differently if you were starting again from scratch? Tell me about some of the specific paperwork reduction initiatives you took. What lessons can other companies learn from your experiences? How has the culture of the organization changed? How did you get people to write more concisely? How did you stop people generating self-protection paperwork? Who were the key players in the campaign? How did you reward people for changing their behaviour? How will you ensure that things don't return to normal in the future?

You will find that after people have attended the exhibition and the workshops there will be a dramatic fall in the volume of paperwork circulating around the office. Reductions of 20–30 per cent are not uncommon in the short term. People begin questioning the 'put it in writing' approach and instead of jealously guarding their own paperwork they start to think about the burden it places on its recipients. As a result documents are briefer, circulation lists are shorter and many items are replaced by direct communication. People also start sitting down with colleagues from other departments to look at ways of simplifying the information paths between them. Even those who were sceptical about the campaign when it was launched will become enthusiastic about it as they see success after success making things better for everyone.

ORGANIZE A CLEAR YOUR DESK! DAY (WEEKS 37–39)

In the planning stages of your paperwork reduction campaign you should designate one date in the calendar to be the organization's annual Clear Your Desk! day. The idea behind the day is that everyone in the organization should stop work for a few hours to clear the dead paperwork from their desks, shelves, filing cabinets, archives and computers. As well as creating an organized working environment the day ensures that every person in the organization becomes involved in the campaign. As people work through their filing cabinets they cannot but ask themselves 'Why did we need to generate this paperwork in the first place?' and this questioning attitude is essential to ensure that the next stage of the campaign, the paperchase, is a success. You should be prepared to collect enormous quantities of dead paperwork on the day – if the day is well organized, you will discard about a tonne of paper for every 50 office workers taking part! It is essential that the day is not seen as a 'tidy up the office' or a 'let's become green and recycle all our junk' day.

The message should be 'let's get organized' rather than 'let's get tidy'.

Your departmental champions should ensure that everything runs smoothly on the day. Arranging for several tonnes of paper to be collected in one place and taken away is quite a task! As filing drawers and cabinets are emptied they should be removed before people have a chance to fill them up again. A team of filing experts should tour the organization's offices giving one-to-one advice on setting up effective filing systems. After the clearout the departmental champions, accompanied by the chief executive, should adopt the role of paper police to ensure that everyone has taken part.

'No! that's just the paperwork from my desk.'

Before the actual day, your campaign team should set legal and commercial retention schedules for the key documents in each department so people can feel confident about discarding non-important paperwork. Where documents are routinely filed in more than one location you should designate one copy as the official copy. Those with non-official copies will feel comfortable about discarding them if they know that the information is readily available else-where. The Clear Your Desk! day should also involve a purge of dead electronic information. The filing maxim 'if you don't know you have it or you can't find it then it's of absolutely no use to you!' applies to electronic documents as well as paper. Everyone taking part in the day should fol-low the action plan below.

CLEAR YOUR DESK! DAY ACTION PLAN

1 Discard all the dead files from your desk, shelves, filing cabinets and computer disks.

2 Reorganize your filing system to minimize the amount of time you spend searching for documents. You can organize your files by date, by subject, by colour, numerically, geographically or alphabetically. Once you have decided on the most suitable classification system relabel your file tabs and folders.

3 Get rid of post-it notes, scraps of paper, jotters, A4 pads, wall planners, and transfer them to one diary system – whether it is paper based or electronic.

4 Set up a bring-forward system. This is a file divided into 31 sections corresponding to the days of the month. If a document arrives on your desk that needs to be deal with on the 13th put it into

the section marked 13 or if a report arrives on
your desk that you need to read on the 20th in
preparation for the meeting on the 21st put it in
the section marked 20. Thus instead of having
stacks of delayed and pending paperwork on the
desk to distract you – with invariably the thing
you need to do today buried and forgotten about
– the bring-forward file tells you the right thing to
do at the right time. Every day you will find a pile
of documents that need to be dealt with on that
day and any you can't deal with should be set a
new deadline and put it in the relevant section of
the file.

5 Sort the paperwork on your desk into four stacks:
   an act-on stack, a pass-on stack, a 'to file' stack and
   a discard stack.

6 Deal with your discard stack by working through
   it and deciding what you need to do to prevent
   each document arriving on your desk in future.
   What circulation lists should you not be on? What
   mailing lists do you want your name removed
   from?

7 Deal with your pass-on stack by deciding who
   needs to deal with each item. If you are delegating
   paperwork or you need information back, agree a
   deadline and make a note of it.

8 Deal with your act-on stack by assigning a priority
   and a deadline to each item and then placing it in
   the relevant section of your bring-forward file.

9 Work through your 'to file' stack by asking yourself How will I remember this document in six months' time? – by name? by date? by subject? – and file accordingly.

10 Get rid of high-rise in-trays. Your desk should not contain more than two trays – an In and an Out tray. If you have stacks of trays marked urgent, action, pending, miscellaneous, priority, they just become convenient storage places for procrastination paperwork.

Once the clearout is complete you should implement a clear-desk policy throughout the organization. While many organizations claim to have such a policy, few operate it effectively. In some offices people reach out and sweep a chaotic pile of papers into the nearest drawer just before they go home each evening. The next morning the pile is retrieved and dumped on the desk again. There is little value in creating the ideal working environment when you are not there to benefit from it! A second type of rogue clear-desk policy involves people keeping their desktops immaculately clear while hiding chaotic piles of paper underneath the desk, in the filing system or in the computer. You will of course face resistance to the clear-desk idea from your bureaucratic colleagues who surround themselves with paper as a way of saying to others 'Look how busy I am, look how hard I'm working!' Each piece of paper lying on the desk however represents a decision we have not yet made or an action we have not yet taken. Cluttered desks and disorganized filing systems lead to unwanted distractions, frantic searches for lost information, missed opportunities and deadlines, unexpected crises and high activity–low-achievement work patterns.

The only way to stay on top of your paperwork and keep your desk relatively clear at all times is to be decisive in dealing with incoming items. There are only four things you can do with a piece of paper – you can act on it, pass it on, file it or bin it! Handling the same bit of paper several times without making a definite decision about what to do with it will ensure that you are extremely busy and extremely unproductive. The measles test provides a good measure of your decisiveness. Each time you pick up a new document put a red dot in the corner. If you pick up the same document again mark it with a second red dot. Then after a week if all the paperwork on your desk and e-mail messages has had an outbreak of measles, you will know how indecisive you are. I strongly recommend the measles test to all my seminar participants as it gives you a very good insight into the number of times you handle the same bit of paper.

CHAPTER FIVE

The Paperchase

'Here's the report you requested on the paperless office!'

The previous four stages were concerned with increasing awareness of the paperwork problem and building support and momentum for the campaign throughout the organization. By now you should have liberated individuals from their bureaucratic mind-set and instilled in them a minimal paper attitude. The time is ripe for the final decisive attack on the information mountain – the paperchase.

THE PAPERCHASE (WEEKS 40–51)

You are now ready to move on to the most important stage of the minimal paper office project – the paperchase. This involves scrutinizing each area of the business to identify and eliminate all non-essential information and paperwork. Members of the campaign team, staff in the particular department being scrutinized and support staff should work through the paperchase checklists below and leave no stone unturned in their efforts to weed out all the Dead, Fat, Dump and Junk documents from the organization.

Staff within each department should be encouraged to actively participate in the paperchase but they should not be given sole responsibility for eliminating their own junk. Day-to-day activities will always demand their attention and it is easy for the project to be pushed aside while more pressing matters are attended to. Members of the campaign team can focus full time on the paperwork problem and also resolve intra- and inter-departmental conflicts. There may be tremendous enthusiasm for the project within a department but if the department head is highly resistant to change and is constantly demanding new forms, new reports and other documentation, there is little his/her subordinates can do to change things. There can also be conflict between departments. One department might insist that it needs certain information, and believes it has a divine right to demand it, while those burdened with the paperwork will argue that their time should be spent elsewhere. Here, again, there would be little change without the campaign team and a consultant working as independent arbitrators.

'It's no use, John — you'll never get away!'

You must recognize that in eliminating paperwork that has been around for many years you are saying to people 'All those long hours and late nights you spent on this paperwork in the past was largely a waste of time.' This can have a dangerous demotivating effect so it is important that the system is blamed rather than individuals. One chief executive in launching the paperchase made the following speech:

> *It's something that I've emphasized from the start of this campaign – the system is at fault rather than individual staff members and I don't want to see anybody being blamed for past sins. God knows I've been just as bad as everyone else at sending out self-congratulatory, FYI and 'cover your ass' junk. If you point the finger at people, it's very demotivating – you're saying to someone who might have put weeks of effort into creating a manual that they are stupid, the work they've been doing has been a complete waste of time. It's much better to say that although this is the way things have worked in the past – you've been encouraged to put things in writing, from now on things will be different. Of course it will be difficult to change because everyone has had years of practice at documenting everything. However, if they learned to adapt to a bureaucratic work environment they can just as easily learn to adapt to a minimal paper one. People will feel a little bit insecure as their comfort blankets are removed but over time they will come to realize that the minimal paper office makes things easier for everyone.*

The paperchase should start in those departments where you are likely to face the least resistance and whose staff have been supporting the campaign from the start. Dramatic results achieved in one area of the business can be held up as an example to others. All the 'it won't work' excuses and bureaucratic myths can be dealt with by pointing to the department where paperwork has been successfully eliminated. No harm can be done by creating a bit of healthy competition between different areas of the business.

PAPERCHASE CHECKLISTS

In working through the checklists below you should bear in mind that your aim is not to save paper but to reduce the time and resources wasted in generating and handling unnecessary paperwork. Allowing the green campaigners to hijack your campaign will deflect attention away from the real issues. If you publicize the campaign with statements like 'our photocopies are the equivalent of 3,000 trees', you will get suggestions like let's photocopy on both sides of the page, let's reuse paper, let's circulate rather than copy, let's make the typeface smaller or let's put it on the computer. The bureaucrats will be delighted and actively support all these proposals because they will reduce paper but fail to reduce the paperwork burden.

Reports paperchase

Most people who generate reports would be shocked if they saw what happened when the product of hours of work landed on the desks of their colleagues. Most reports are ignored, glanced at for a few seconds and then left aside or thrown straight in the bin. Even the person who requested the report in the first place often has no use for it. When asking for the report what they really meant to say was 'go away' I'm busy right now!' As you work through the list of ad hoc and routine reports generated within the organization, ask the recipients the following questions:

1 Is this report always read all the way through?
2 Who should be removed from the circulation list?
3 Does this report affect the decisions the recipients make?
4 Would the recipients be able to get this information elsewhere?
5 Should this report be generated less frequently?
6 Would the recipients be satisfied with a report summary?
7 Should the exception reporting principle be used?
8 Could this report be more concise?
9 Should this report be made available only on request?
10 If the recipients had to pay for this report would they still want it?

Document	Conquer the Information Mountain! REPORTS PAPERCHASE	By	Date	Annual savings Paper	Time
1. Sales report	1. Take T. Grant, C. Stone, J. Simpson off circulation list 2. Send one page summaries only, to D. Clark, J. Coates 3. Present information verbally using overheads at monthly mgr's meetings instead of circulating.	D.T.	26/1 28/2 1/3	2,868	112 hrs.
2. Daily production report	1. Send to R. Mandeville, F. Mizen weekly instead of daily 2. Only send to J. Roberts if production falls below 200 3. Place report on server for product mgrs. instead of circulating	A.G.	26/1 26/1 15/4	17,915	600hrs.
3. Client update report	Scrap it! Nobody on the circulation list looks at it. They already have the information that is relevant to them.	A.G.	26/1	1,600	48hrs.

Junk mail paperchase

Unsolicited mail would not be a problem if we threw it straight in the bin. Most of my seminar attendees claim to be ruthless in discarding junk but a quick look at their desks usually reveals a different story. While a certain amount goes straight in the bin there is a significant proportion that gets the response 'oh, that looks interesting!' or 'I'll look at that when I get the time' and remains on the desk. Then when we are procrastinating about tackling some 'real' work, these leaflets and brochures usually get our attention. For this reason prevention is better than cure in conquering the junk mail mountain. Ask a group of people in each department to collect all the junk mail they use over the period of one month and then work through the stack asking the following questions:

1. Do people ask telesales callers to 'send me some information'?
2. Do magazines we subscribe to sell their circulation lists to third parties?
3. Do trade associations sell our names on to others for mailing purposes?
4. Do staff hand out their business cards to suppliers at exhibitions?
5. If we no longer do business with a supplier do we ask to be removed from their mailing lists?
6. Do people have their names listed in directories that are used to compile mailing lists?
7. Is unsolicited mail returned to sender?
8. Do we give out names to telesales callers compiling mailing lists?
9. Do people have their mail screened?
10. Do we generate what others would consider to be junk mail?

Document	Conquer the Information Mountain! JUNK MAIL PAPERCHASE	By	Date	Annual savings Paper	Time
1. Trade Yearbooks	Remove all names from yearbooks they are only used for direct mail purposes.	R.C.	1/4	10,000	300 hrs.
2. Mailing list compilers	Stop giving out names to sales callers.	R.C.	26/1	4,000	120hrs.
3. Magazine Subscriptions	Ask publishers not to sell names on to third parties	C.M.	15/4	1,500	50hrs.

Correspondence paperchase

Invite a group of customers to your offices for an afternoon and go through all the paperwork they have to handle as a result of doing business with you. You will learn more in a few hours talking to people face-to-face than you would learn from sending out thousands of customer satisfaction surveys. Unlike the organization's staff, its customers don't have to put up with being bombarded with bureaucratic paperwork, they can always go elsewhere. Hold a similar session with suppliers and try to identify the Dead, Fat, Dump and Junk information flowing between you.

1 Is this document actually read by the recipient?
2 Does the recipient consider this paperwork to be an unnecessary burden?
3 Is this document fatter than necessary?
4 Would it be possible to reduce the frequency of this correspondence?
5 Is this paperwork sometimes more of a hindrance than a help?

6 Could this paperwork be simplified to make it more user-friendly?

7 Could the matter be dealt with over the phone?

8 Could the paperwork be reduced by dealing with the recipient face-to-face?

9 Could the job be done without this paperwork?

10 Could we reduce the number of people who handle this paperwork?

Document	Conquer the Information Mountain! Seminars CORRESPONDENCE PAPERCHASE	By	Date	Annual savings Paper	Time
1. Information Pack	Reduce information pack from nine separate documents (300 pages) to one (50 pages).	P.M.	31/1	500,000	1,400hrs.
2. Customer Complaints Correspondence	Deal with complaints verbally rather than asking customer to fill in paperwork.	A.J.	1/3	3,000	200hrs.
3. Written Confirmations	Stop written confirmations of conversations both incoming and outgoing.	C.R.	1/4	60,,000	2,000hrs.

Photocopy paperchase

Each department should have a specific photocopy reduction target. Remember, the aim of the paperwork reduction campaign is to save work not paper so photocopying on two sides of a piece of paper or circulating instead of copying is not the answer. Set up a team of photocopy police and despatch them to the various copiers around your offices. Anyone approaching the photocopier should be asked the following questions:

1 Could you do without a copy?

2 Do you need to make so many copies?

3 Is there an alternative way of getting the message

across?

4 Do you really need more than one copy for your files?

5 Is a photocopy reminder necessary?

6 Do people really value your 'for your information' copies?

7 Does the recipient already have a copy?

8 Could you use the notice-board for this information?

9 Could you reduce the circulation list?

10 Could you edit the document to make it more concise?

Document	Conquer the Information Mountain! PHOTOCOPY PAPERCHASE	By	Date	Annual savings Paper	Time
1. Admin. Dept. Photocopier	Cut the number of photocopiers in the Admin. Dept. from five to four.	A.J.	1/4	50,000	500 hrs.
2. FYI photocopies	Copies should only be sent to those who need to take action.	D.T.	26/1	18,000	250hrs.
3. Photocopy Reminders	Missed deadlines should be followed up verbally	D.T.	15/4	4,000	200hrs.

Files and records paperchase

Your colleagues will have already discarded tonnes of paper from their files during the Clear Your Desk! day but there will still be room for improvement. Members of the project team along with records management experts should examine the paper and electronic filing systems in each department in order to identify dead or duplicate files. The following questions should be asked:

1 Is this information ever used?

2 Is there a copy of this document stored elsewhere?

3 Who should be responsible for filing the official copy of this document?

4 Is the cost of keeping this document greater than the cost of not keeping it?

5 Will you ever have time to read this document?

6 Do you need to keep the complete document or just part of it?

7 Should this document be filed centrally?

8 Should this document be archived or just thrown away?

9 Is this document stored electronically?

10 For how long do we need to retain this document?

Document	Conquer the Information Mountain! FILES & RECORDS PAPERCHASE	By	Date	Annual savings Paper	Time
1. Retention Schedules	*Establish legal and retention schedules for all files and discard all dead files.*	A.J.	1/4	**2,000,000**	**3,500 hrs.**
2. Duplicate files	*Designate certain files as official copies and determine who is responsible for keeping them.*	A.J.	1/4	**1,500,000**	**2,000hrs.**
3. File Conversion	*Cut conversion of junk paper files to electronic format.*	C.R.	28/3	**500,000**	**10,000hrs.**

Manuals paperchase

I knew I was in for a tough time on one consulting assignment when the administration manager pulled a weighty volume from a shelf groaning under the weight of dusty documents. It was the in-house manual on how to write manuals! A classic example of a manual produced because its author had nothing else to do!

Most manuals try to cover every contingency and eventuality and are consequently ignored because they are too complicated. It is far better to cut out the waffle and concentrate on the key points – more people will be aware of what they are and if they have a problem they can always ask someone else what to do. Take each manual in turn and ask those it is supposed to help the following questions:

1 What would be the worst thing that could happen if this manual was scrapped?
2 How often do people refer to the manual?
3 Does the manual tell people what they already know?
4 Could this manual be simplified?
5 Is the perceived value of the manual greater than the cost of producing and maintaining it?
6 Does every possible contingency and eventuality need to be covered?
7 Is there a more effective way of getting the message across?
8 Who needs a copy of this manual?
9 Does the manual give rise to secondary paperwork?

Conquer the Information Mountain!		🚶	🕐	Annual savings 💰	
Document	**MANUALS PAPERCHASE**	By	Date	Paper	Time
1. Personnel Manual	It's too complicated – reduce by 50 per cent	H.R.	1/4	*150,000*	*350 hrs.*
2. Sales Procedures Manual	Reduce down to one page and include only the key points.	R.G.	26/1	*90,000*	*180hrs.*
3. Contracts Manual	Simplify manual – especially related forms and paperwork.	J.S.	30/8	*130,000*	*800hrs.*

10 Does the manual encourage people to act in a bureaucratic way?

Standard forms paperchase

Many of the forms used within your organization will
undoubtedly be helpful but there will also be a long list of
forms that are over-bureaucratic and whose handling costs
are greater than the value of the information they collect.
The trouble with superfluous forms is that once introduced
they create an unwanted burden again and again. Once you
have identified and eliminated all the unnecessary forms
you should use the 'one in, one out' principle. Before any
new form is introduced a form already in use must be eliminated. Starting with those forms that generate the most
paperwork ask everyone who handles them the following
questions:

1 Is the form obsolete?
2 Could the form be redesigned to make it more user-
friendly?
3 Does the information asked for by the form already
exist elsewhere?
4 Do people find this form more of a hindrance than a
help?
5 Could this form be merged with another one?
6 Should this form be simplified?
7 Is all the information asked for by this form actually
used?
8 Can the number of people who currently handle this
form be reduced?

9 Are all the copies of this form really necessary?
10 Is the cost of collecting and storing this information greater than its value?
11 Could the information be obtained by word of mouth?

Document	Conquer the Information Mountain! STANDARD FORMS PAPERCHASE	By	Date	Annual savings Paper	Time
1. Telephone Extension Change Form	*Using these forms is unnecessarily bureaucratic and they have brought no benefits since their introduction.*	A.T.	1/4	*800*	*200 hrs.*
2. Training Evaluation Forms	*Nobody ever looks at them. Talking to the participants builds up a better picture.*	A.T.	30/1	*11,000*	*1,800hrs.*
3. Sales Activity Forms	*The information in these forms is available from other sources.*	R.G.	30/1	*15,000*	*2,500hrs.*

Memo paperchase

Unfortunately a great many of the memos that arrive on our desks tell us things that we already know or that we didn't need to know. Because memos are one-off documents people need to be encouraged to get out of the 'memo habit'. Ask people in each department to collect all the unnecessary memos and e-mail messages they receive for one month and then go through them asking the following questions.

1 Is this memo really necessary?
2 Does this memo tell the reader something they already know?
3 Could this information have been communicated by other means?

4 Should this memo have been sent to someone else?
5 Did the recipient need to take action on this memo?
6 Are there too many cc.s on the memo?
7 Is this memo as concise as it should be?
8 Would a quick conversation have been a better way of getting the message across?
9 Would a handwritten note have sufficed?
10 Is this memo reader protective rather than writer effective?

Document	Conquer the Information Mountain! Seminar MEMO PAPERCHASE	By	Date	Annual savings Paper	Time
1. E-mail	Stop confirmation of conversations via e-mail.	A.H.	1/4	120,000	300 hrs.
2. FYI Memos	Send memos only to those who need to take action.	M.B.	26/1	250,000	480hrs.
3. Fat Memos	Restrict all memos to one page or less.	J.T.	30/1	170,000	400hrs.

Having worked through the paperchase checklists a one-page paperwork reduction action list should be produced for every department. It should be framed and displayed in a prominent place to serve as a constant reminder of the commitments people have made. The total volume of paperwork to be eliminated should be calculated and each paperwork reduction suggestion should have a sponsor and an implementation deadline. The campaign team should be vigilant in ensuring that the early deadlines are met because if they are allowed to slip at this stage, longer-term initiatives just won't be implemented. If any one department is not meeting its targets the campaign team will need to work closely with them to get the project back on track and if necessary call on the chief executive to pay a short, sharp, shock visit.

Once you have identified the minimum amount of information necessary to run the business you should now concentrate on the question – should this information be electronic or on paper? Only where people would prefer it to be in digital format should your IT people be brought in. Allowing them to take over the process earlier will mean that lots of junk paper will be converted to junk information. Chasing the paperless office goal deflects attention away from the real issues – eliminating the bureaucratic behaviour that creates unnecessary paperwork in soft- and hard-copy formats.

REVIEW THE CAMPAIGN (WEEKS 51–52)

The final stage of the campaign is to review its progress to date to confirm that paperwork reduction and culture-change targets have been reached. Achieving the minimal paper office is a process that will take several years so a 5–10 per cent paperwork reduction target should be set for year two of the campaign. You may well have already identified a number of areas of the business that need to be rescrutinized in a more ruthless fashion.

Throughout the campaign department heads should be regularly asked to report to the paperwork reduction team on its progress within their departments. Once the project is complete each area of the business should be asked to prepare a brief presentation on their achievements for the chief executive and the board. These presentations should focus on the incoming paperwork that has been simplified or eliminated, the outgoing paperwork that has been simplified or eliminated, the paperwork reductions that will occur in the future, the cost savings, productivity benefits, staff morale benefits, the customer and supplier benefits. Knowing that this presentation has to be made keeps people focused on results throughout the campaign.

Once you are confident that your paperwork reduction campaign has been an outstanding success you should start shouting about it. You should apply for a PAPERWORK REDUCTION AWARD which is presented to those organizations that have declared war on paperwork and won. Used on your streamlined electronic and paper documentation it signifies a long-term commitment to conducting business in a non-bureaucratic way. You should also let your PR people loose on the press to publicize your efforts as a reputation for efficiency can only inspire confidence amongst shareholders, customers, suppliers and members of the general public. The following article was printed in a trade magazine bringing considerable kudos to the organization involved. You should aim for a similar write-up.

UBC CONQUER THE INFORMATION MOUNTAIN!

Twelve months ago UBC's staff were buried under a mountain of paperwork and electronic information. Chief executive Ron Goodman decided enough was enough and launched a paperwork reduction drive. The company discarded 140 tonnes of dead paperwork from its files and this year will circulate 4 million fewer reports, forms, memos and manuals. Goodman personally helped to carry 30 filing cabinets out of the office so they wouldn't fill up with paper again. Joan Fielding went to investigate.

In advance of corporate visits I usually receive a two-inch thick press pack from some terribly nice PR person. Although I never read them I don't throw them away as they make useful stands for the coffee cups on my desk and my editor thinks I am frightfully busy. UBC's PR manager Fiona Rodford refused to send me a single scrap of paper, telling me they were trying to cut down on the burden of paperwork they placed on others. I was intrigued.

Goodman met me in reception and immediately drew my attention to a plaque on the wall – it was a paperwork reduction award presented to the organization for eliminating the equivalent of 800 miles of paperwork. I mischievously asked him how much he had invested in computer technology to get rid of all the paperwork. (We've gone down the paperless route in our magazine office and are now knee-deep in electronic information.) Goodman, however, pointed out that he had seen other organizations he worked for falling into the same trap and that UBC's goal was to eliminate all junk information regardless of whether it was on paper or on the computer.

Early on in their campaign UBC staff spent an afternoon with a group of customers, asking them to place a value on the paperwork they received from the company. They found that much of it was considered to be unnecessary and with its subsequent elimination customers now find it much easier to deal with the company. As the company bombarded its staff and customers with excess paperwork the cost of preprinted paperwork in the form of letterheads, leaflets, forms, manuals and brochures decreased by a very satisfactory 60 per cent. The company's mailing costs also dropped by 32 per cent.

Goodman stressed the importance of getting staff at all levels involved in the campaign. He personally invited a bureaucracy-bashing consultant to run Conquer the Information Mountain! workshops for all of the company's 800 staff. Goodman also gave me a guided tour of an exhibition which was originally set up to highlight the organization's bureaucratic excesses but now highlights its many paperwork reduction successes. The company whittled down its 187 standard forms to a more respectable 38 and in the process eliminated 2,000,000 sheets of paper. Reports were also examined and as a result 1,350,000 fewer sheets of paper are generated annually but more importantly 80,000 hours have been freed up that people spent handling them.

The total cost savings as a result of Goodman's campaign were in excess of £1,350,000. The stationery budget was reduced by 45 per cent. The costs of purchasing, leasing and maintaining photocopiers and computer printers was reduced by 25 per cent per annum. Goodman also put a halt on a proposed purchase of 86 printers (a total investment of £165,000) and said if we generate less junk we can get by with what we already have because more printers will mean more junk.

When I asked Goodman what lessons others could learn from his experiences he said his own minimal paper philosophy could be applied to any organization – it is based on two commonsense principles, keep it simple and take talk seriously. He also reeled off ten critical success factors for companies wishing to achieve the minimal paper office.

10 CRITICAL SUCCESS FACTORS

1 Assign credible, action-oriented staff to your campaign team. ❑

2 Ensure that senior management openly support the campaign. ❑

3 Set a specific paperwork reduction target. ❑

4 Recognize and reward those who adopt a 'minimal paper' attitude. ❑

5 Use outside expertise to help you break out of your bureaucratic mind-set. ❑

6 Ensure that all staff attend Conquer the Information Mountain! seminars. ❑

7 Prevent the campaign being hijacked by those with green or IT agendas. ❑

8 Change all the paperwork generated by every

department. ❏

9 Allocate sufficient resources to make the campaign a success. ❏

10 Allay fears that the campaign will lead to job losses. ❏

CHAPTER SIX

The Paperwork Reduction Principles

'I've got the paperwork reduction commandments – make 5,000 copies straight away!'

A client of mine spent a week visiting an organization which had already made considerable progress on the journey towards the minimal paper office. In trying to spot what was different he at first wandered around counting the paper on people's desks until he realized that there might be a mountain of bureaucratic forms and memos hidden in the computer. After several days he came across the answer:

Listening to conversations in corridors or at meetings you continually hear evidence of the minimal paper culture. Whereas back in our offices people generate Dead, Fat, Dump and Junk paperwork out of force of habit, here people were constantly speaking out to ensure that no unnecessary documents were generated. During the week I spent there I heard hundreds of comments such as the following. 'There's no need to confirm that in writing, I'll get on to it straight away', 'don't send me a memo on it, go and sort out the problem and then tell me what you've done', 'could you keep the report less than two pages – I fall asleep if I have to read anything longer', 'well, if we're going to introduce this new form we'll have to get rid of something else first otherwise they won't have time to do their proper jobs!' and 'we don't need to have an instruction booklet if we go and show people how to do the

job!' These seemingly unimportant comments prevented thou-
sands of pieces of unnecessary paper being generated.

The changes that need to take place to shift your organization's culture from a 'put it in writing' to a 'minimal paper' one
can be encapsulated in a set of guidelines – the paperwork
reduction principles. Whereas the bureaucratic myths we
looked at in Chapter Three were the foundation on which the
information mountain was built, the paperwork reduction
principles form the foundations for the minimal paper office.

THE PAPERWORK REDUCTION PRINCIPLES

- Justify it or scrap it!
- KISS!
- GOYA!
- Take talk seriously!
- Action not paperwork!
- Hands off!
- AOR!
- One in–one out!
- Speak out!
- Be brief!

These principles should be regarded as a set of rules that
apply to everyone and everything. They should be adopted
with nothing short of religious zeal – just knowing what
they are will not change anything. A die-hard bureaucrat
once stood up during one of my seminars and asked: 'Why
are you wasting our time telling us all this KISS and "take
talk seriously" stuff – we already know it?' The chief

executive who was present replied to the question for me. He pulled several fat memos, previously circulated by the manager, from a pile of papers in front of him and said 'if you really know it then why aren't you doing it?'

Justify it or scrap it!

The justify it or scrap it principle demands that you constantly question the value of all the paperwork you circulate to and demand from others. Any document whose pay-off doesn't justify the time spent handling it should be eliminated.

Don't underestimate the difficulty of applying this principle successfully. As one minimal paper office project manager pointed out, we can clearly spot others' bad paperwork but when our own documents are questioned our judgement becomes cloudy.

We had great difficulty in getting people to apply the principle to their own paperwork. At the start of the campaign everyone was complaining about the stuff arriving on their desks and they were saying to me 'Personnel, marketing, finance can't possibly justify that, tell them to scrap it.' It took us a while to get the message across that the principle is not there to be applied to other people's paperwork but to your own. Initially of course people used every bureaucratic myth in the book when justifying their own paperwork but gradually they realized that they weren't going to lose their jobs if they eliminated things.

As well as having difficulty in getting people to focus on their own paperwork you will find it hard to get them to be ruthless enough in their evaluation of what is essential. In most organizations paperwork reduction campaigns focus on the 'easy' paperwork such as photocopies or e-mail messages. The 'difficult' paperwork such as forms, manuals and reports that have always been around is usually ignored. To ensure that the justify or scrap it principle is adopted you will need to get the message across very early in the paperwork reduction campaign so that no stone will be left unturned in the identification and elimination of unnecessary paperwork. A hit-list of documents that are generally accepted to be essential should be compiled. These documents should then be put under the microscope by asking questions such as What is the worst thing that would happen if this document was eliminated? Could we live with the consequences? How could we simplify things to eliminate this document? What is the alternative? If we were starting from scratch, would be need this? If you are ruthless enough you will find that a number of these supposedly essential documents can be eliminated without any harmful effects. If you can get rid of this type of paperwork then the message to everyone is loud and clear – nothing is sacred!

People will have a natural tendency to err on the side of caution in questioning the usefulness of their paperwork and many documents will be retained 'just in case'. The 'if in doubt, throw it out' approach should be therefore be promoted – it's not as frivolous as you may think. If you get rid of any bit of paper and you make a mistake you can always bring it back! However, unless you get rid of it on a trial basis you will never really know if it was necessary in the first place. Ruthlessness should come from the top down with senior managers occasionally tearing up memos or ceremoniously dumping non-essential manuals or forms. If those at the top are not prepared to demonstrate such ruthlessness then those further down the organization can hardly be expected to develop a questioning attitude to their own paperwork.

KISS

The KISS principle (Keep It Simple, Stupid) states that you should always find the easiest way of doing the job well! In bureaucratic organizations people find it difficult to get things done in a straightforward fashion. The simplest of processes cannot be completed without a barrage of e-mail messages, forms and other bits of paper. Much of this paperwork has been created for self-protection purposes in response to one-off problems that have occurred over the years. The following statements may sound familiar to you. 'I received a phone call from the MD and I hadn't a clue what was going on. Please copy me in on all correspondence in future' or 'It's not our fault! Bill says he can't remember your, asking him to send you the goods. In future you'll have to fill in a form so we have a written record of what was requested.'

As well as new paperwork clogging up processes, individual documents such as forms, manuals and reports tend to grow in complexity over time. With forms the thinking seems to be 'well, as we have the form in place we might as well use it to collect this extra information' or 'let's put a few extra boxes on the form to check that the new procedure is followed.' We all know that KISS forms, KISS reports, KISS memos and KISS manuals take less time to generate and impose less of a bureaucratic burden on their recipients but few of us take positive steps to reverse the trend towards increasing complexity. The marketing manager of a media company recounts how they adopted the KISS principle:

We were adapt at making the simple things complicated and the complicated things impossible. You couldn't get anything done without having to fill in the paperwork. We identified over a 100 separate forms being used on a daily basis throughout the company. In addition there were 40,000 memos circulated every year which meant that one landed on somebody's desk every two minutes. People just had to have a bit of paper to prove that if something went wrong it wasn't their fault. We had 30 stamps made up and each one had a pair of lips surrounded by the words 'apply the KISS principle!' We handed them out to one department and asked people to stamp every piece of paper they felt was too complex. Not surprisingly about 70 per cent of the documents that passed across people's desks failed the KISS test. We collected all these documents together and decided what needed to be done to simplify things. Other departments saw what was going on and demanded KISS stamps for their paperwork. Even now, five years later, if people see complicated documents they pull out the KISS stamp — we have introduced an electronic version as well.

GOYA

The Get Off Your Ass principle is quite clear in encouraging people not to bury their head in paperwork but to go and talk to people if they need to collect or disseminate information. Adopting this principle means that your management style will change from a paper-orientated to a people-oriented one.

'He likes to catch up on his paperwork in the afternoons!'

From time to time we all get stuck in bureaucratic mode – sending out written instructions, developing new forms, generating and requesting reports instead of communicating directly with people. A vicious cycle can then be created where we are so busy replying to the written responses to our original paperwork that we don't have time to leave our desks and find out what is really going on around us. In the long-run direct contact with others builds relationships and trust, increasing the chances of things getting done, while putting it in writing creates a climate of mistrust, increases paperwork and lowers productivity. An enforced desk ban as decreed by one chief executive can sometimes be the only way to break out of that cycle:

Our managers spent every working hour stuck at their desks filling in paperwork. They became expert paper shufflers but hadn't a clue what was going on around them. We placed a ban on managers spending more than an hour a day at their desks for one month and forced them to go and talk to production staff and people they never knew existed before — customers! The volume of memos, forms and ad hoc reports dropped by 70 per cent during the month and yet our managers said they had gathered more valuable information than usual about what was happening in the company.

TAKE TALK SERIOUSLY!

The 'Take Talk Seriously' principle states that verbal communication should carry as much weight as written communication. Many people erroneously believe that intrays piled high with memos, reports, newsletters and staff surveys signify good communication throughout the organization. The mountain of paper however is much more likely to signify that communication between colleagues has completely broken down!

When you are surrounded by bureaucratic slogans such as 'if it's not written down it doesn't exist!' and every conversation seems to end with the words 'would you put that in writing!', it's easy to forget that verbal communication has many advantages over the printed word. For a start talking is more natural than writing. In conversation the words flow naturally whereas when writing we are inhibited by thoughts of what to say, how to say it and how to spell it. If speed is of the essence then talking is the best form of communication — a quick conversation can get things going while sitting down and writing a memo and waiting for someone to read and respond to it can take days or even weeks. Talking is also a more powerful means of communication because of the range of tools, such as facial expression, gestures, tone of voice, volume and posture, we can use to enrich the communication. Talking is also a two-way communication which means we can answer questions and adjust our message according to the audience's reaction to our message. As one manager discovered, the battle to conquer the information mountain is as much a battle to promote good verbal communication as it is to eliminate excess written communication:

For the past decade we have been chasing the paperless office and worrying about how to convert our stacks of paper into electronic format. Now we've changed and are saying 'let's get rid of what is unnecessary and let's talk more!' Implementing the Take Talk Seriously has meant an end to all those confirmation memos, copious meeting minutes and bureaucratic checklists. Our fat reports have also been replaced by verbal presentations. Of course there is occasionally a misunderstanding but when we look back there were just as many misunderstandings with written communication and we now waste a lot less time pushing paper! Before if people were asked to do something they might agree but would wait until someone sat down and confirmed it in writing. We've now turned the tables around and instead of saying 'I can't act unless I have it in writing' we encourage people to send memos back to senders and say 'I can't act unless you come and ask me'.

ACTION NOT PAPERWORK

The 'Action Not Paperwork' principle states that if something goes wrong you should focus your energies on solving the problem rather than writing about it. As the manager below recounts, paperwork is a great way of keeping busy without actually getting anything done.

We got into a situation where if something went wrong the knee-jerk reaction was 'let's write a report on it!' or 'we need to invent a form to monitor the situation!' We were generating lots of paperwork which was being used to avoid making decisions or taking action – instead the problem was shuffled

on to someone else's desk. All this paperwork was just a drain on time and resources and did little to help in solving the problem. In fact our first abortive attempt at a paperwork reduction campaign involved a task force from HR and IT who spent three months looking at the problem and then produced a 200-page report. There are scores of copies of that report gathering dust in people's filing systems, mostly unread. We'd spent hundreds of hours writing about what we should do instead of doing it. The one thing that changed everything was when the chief executive received a three-page memo from one of the department heads about a customer problem. It was something that should have been sorted out quite quickly. He walked into the manager's office, tore up the memo and asked him why he was wasting his time generating paperwork when there was an unhappy customer waiting to be dealt with.

HANDS OFF!

The 'Hands Off' principle insists that documents should be handled by the minimum number of people! In the bureaucratic office there is very much a 'hands on' approach with a tendency for too many people to be involved in generating and handling documents. A form that could be processed by one person will often land on half a dozen desks: a memo that requires action by one person will be circulated to several people and a report that contains information relevant to one department will be circulated throughout the organization. As one finance manager points out, the paperwork reduction campaign is about ensuring that the minimum amount of paperwork is generated and that this paperwork is then handled by the minimum number of people.

We had one manager who insisted on editing and re-editing all her subordinates' correspondence which was a complete waste of time. We had one report which was generated by one manager and circulated to all the department heads. Someone in head office regurgitated the information in a separate report and circulated it to everyone as well. There was nothing in the second report that wasn't contained in the first. People would often respond to memos that should never have been sent to them in the first place and every form had to go round the houses to be authorized. We went through all our horizontal and vertical paper trails and asked why can't one person or at most two people handle this document? Are we duplicating work that has already been done elsewhere? We also got people to ask themselves should someone else be doing this job? Would the job get done without the paperwork passing across my desk? If the answer was yes then we told people to leave the paperwork alone.

AOR!

The 'AOR' (Available On Request) principle is clear. Instead of firing out information indiscriminately, tell people where they can find it *if* they need it. This principle applies to the mass of routine information such as reports, memos, newsletters, updates and press cuttings that are circulated throughout the organization 'just in case' someone might be interested. Even when the information is clearly unnecessary recipients will not take their names off circulation lists for fear of causing offence or sending out the message that they are not interested in what's going on. The bureaucrats will argue that people can just ignore the infor-

'He likes to make sure everyone gets a copy of his memos!'

mation if it is not relevant to them but, as the manager below, laments this avalanche of unnecessary information often deflects attention away from what's important.

We were circulating about two million pages of reports, surveys, product manuals, training updates and PR circulars annually and we found that 60 per cent of it was wasted. People were just firing out information in all directions hoping someone would find it useful. There was so much information flying about that even the valuable paperwork was buried and ignored under piles of junk on people's desks. We introduced the AOR principle for almost all of our personnel, marketing, and training information by putting it on the computer for people to access it as and when required. We've also used the AOR principle during meetings –

instead of people handing out great wodges of background paperwork before the meeting, fat handouts during the meeting and copious minutes afterwards, people were told where to find these things if they wanted them. We stopped more than a million pieces of paper arriving on people's desks every year.

ONE IN–ONE OUT

The one in–one out principle recognizes that as a business and its environment change over time then new information and paperwork systems become necessary. However the principle also recognizes the importance of not allowing the paperwork burden to increase, so before any new paperwork is introduced then something else must go. Unless you can identify and eliminate obsolete or low payoff paperwork then the new document must be put on hold. As one sales manager pointed out there is a constant drive to generate new information in organizations and unless you invest time and effort in eliminating what is redundant, your colleagues will be buried under unmanageable quantities of paperwork.

We had a new computer system producing every type of report imaginable and head office administration staff were demanding more and more information from the salespeople to feed into the computer. We estimated that the salespeople's in-trays had doubled in size during the previous three years. Many of them just couldn't cope with the paperwork burden and their sales suffered as they sought to get all the paperwork done. We introduced the one in–one out principle by saying to our administration people 'Our salespeople should be spending

*no more than four hours a week on paperwork so if you want
to introduce new paperwork and it is going to add half an
hour to someone's workload then you will have to reduce their
paper workload by half an hour elsewhere.' The avalanche of
new paperwork was reduced down to a trickle and we got rid
of a lot of stuff that was obsolete.*

SPEAK OUT!

You should not suffer in silence when colleagues are dumping unnecessary paperwork on your desk – ask them to stop
sending it! The 'Speak Out' principle puts the onus on you
the recipient rather than the sender to stem the flow of
unnecessary paperwork. A simple comment such as 'That
report is well put together but we already get the information from the monthly sales report!' or 'We could fill in this
form but marketing already have that information and you
could get it directly from them' will reduce the inflow of
unnecessary paperwork without causing offence to its gen-
erator. In the absence of feedback information producers
often don't realize that their paperwork is considered to be
superfluous and therefore can't be blamed for continuing to
churn it out. The Speak Out principle should not be seen
as an excuse to complain about your colleagues in other
departments but as an opportunity to work with them
constructively to eliminate Dead, Fat, Dump and Junk
paperwork.

*When we first promoted the Speak Out principle people saw
it as an opportunity to whinge to their colleagues about the
amount of unnecessary paperwork arriving on their desks*

from other departments. We had to make it clear to everyone that the principle involves giving constructive feedback to the information producers in order to eliminate the bad paperwork. If someone is sending you a report every month that you never read and you don't ask for your name to be removed from the circulation list then you've nobody to blame but yourself. If you get junk from outside the organization you can throw it straight in the bin and it involves no cost. However if you're binning the internal stuff without saying anything, it means that someone in the organization is wasting our time and money circulating paperwork. We also had a problem where people were keen to speak out about other people's paperwork but were very defensive when it came to others speaking out about their own paperwork. For the principle to work you have go to listen to constructive feedback and take on board what people are saying.

BE BRIEF!

The Be Brief principle demands that you be considerate to those who are on the receiving end of your paperwork. If you absolutely have to 'put it in writing', don't overburden your colleagues with more information than they need! We have all experienced the frustration of wading through fat memos and reports, wishing the author would just get to the point. However, when we generate documents for others we forget that frustration and repeat the same long-winded mistakes.

Being brief does not mean playing the paperholic games of reducing the size of the text, the number of paragraphs or the line spacing. Being brief is about cutting out unnecessary information and editing your writing to make it more clear and concise. The experience of all organizations who are obsessive about the 'Be Brief!' principle is that concise documents are more likely to be read and actioned. With more and more information arriving on our desks all the time our attention spans are decreasing. A decade ago we might have been able to spend a couple of hours poring over the monthly report whereas now there is a three-foot stack of reports beckoning to be read. It should also be noted that the higher up the organization your audience, the more important it is to be brief. The psychologists tell us why.

A child of 6–10 months has only a very brief attention span. At that age the child will only focus on an object for a few seconds before its attention wanes and something else more interesting is sought out. When the child starts school at age five its attention span has increased to about two minutes and by the time it reaches its early teenage years attention span has increased to 20 minutes. Research has shown that as you move up through the organization hierarchy attention spans move in the opposite direction. A supervisor will typically have an attention span of about 20 minutes while the in-tray of a department head is considerably higher and will result in a lower attention span of about 10 minutes. At senior management level attention span has decreased to two minutes or less because of the sheer volume of information arriving on the desk. If you haven't grabbed the reader's attention in that time, your ideas and recommendations will be ignored. The lesson to be learned is quite clear: if you want your writing to have impact at senior level – write for the five-year-olds running your business!

'Do you want to read this report, Timmy — or shall I file it?'

CHAPTER SEVEN

Conquer the Information
Mountain! Case Study

In many instances people lose sight of what they are there to do!
Previously people saw work as processing administration – they did not
see that standing there appearing to do nothing but looking for
customers to serve was the primary reason why they were employed.

Marks & Spencer is renowned worldwide for its Good Housekeeping campaign in the late 1950s when, under the stewardship of Simon Marks, the company launched an attack on bureaucracy and paperwork in a bid to curb the rise in administrative expenses. As a result of the campaign the company rid itself of 26 million sheets of unnecessary paper and sold off more than 1,000 filing cabinets which were no longer required. An exhibition set up to highlight the company's success in eliminating waste was visited by over 10,000 business people from all over the world.

In 1992 the chairman, Sir Richard Greenbury, and the board, became convinced that Marks & Spencer was once again becoming excessively bureaucratic. They were concerned that the information mountain was diverting people's attention away from the 'real work' of the business – buying and selling merchandise. In the words of one Marks & Spencer director, 'We had lost sight of the importance of keeping our operations simple and non-bureaucratic. We had developed bad habits and practices which resulted in enormous volumes of paperwork and information being created, circulated and stored. Very little of it was essential to the efficient running of the business and much of it added no value whatsoever.'

As a result of these concerns the 'Business Review of Information and Paperwork' was initiated to leave 'no stone unturned' in the bid to reduce the paperwork burden and eliminate wasteful practices. Prior to 1992 the company had undertaken over 50 short-term 'scrutinies' which involved the board identifying a topic of concern which was investigated by a senior manager over a six-week period. A report was compiled laying out a plan of action which was then implemented by line management. While the scrutiny approach was responsible for many improvements within the business it was felt to be unsuitable for the war against paperwork. Those conducting the scrutiny would neither have enough time to examine the paperwork generated by all areas of the business and they would have to accept everything they were told at face value. Sir Richard Greenbury believed that a more rigorous and long-lasting campaign was needed to get to grips with the information mountain – and with a vision that a Marks & Spencer store could be operated with just six pieces of paper his expectations were high!

The Business Review of Information and Paperwork was thus launched to be conducted in two phases. The first phase covered the flow of communication to and from the network of 300 stores and internal mail within head office while the second, starting six months later, focused on internal processes within all head office working groups. It was recognized that to be successful the review needed to be led by the sharp end of the business rather than given to a support department such as administration or audit. A director was nominated to sponsor each phase of the review and a full-time team of four experienced managers with secretarial support was then assembled. The team members were fast-track people who could ill afford to be released from their normal jobs and this further emphasized the importance of the review.

The review was launched with a one-page briefing being sent to all levels of management. This document reiterated many of the principles which had made the Good Housekeeping campaign a success in the 1950s. Tough targets were set for the review with Sir Richard demanding a 25 per cent reduction in circulating paperwork over the next year. This was to be followed by a further 5 per cent reduction in each of the three subsequent years. As a result of the campaign the company expected to cut its operating costs by about £10 million.

The Review

It is generally accepted that the volume of information and paperwork in our business has become burdensome and wasteful of the time and effort of some of our staff. The review will challenge the need for all information and paperwork in the business. It will eliminate non-essential information and divert the efforts of people to more productive tasks.

Objectives

- To identify the minimum information and frequency required to do the essential work
- To eliminate that which is not essential

- To simplify and rationalize the creation, flow and storage of information making full use of existing systems
- To ensure that the gains identified are exploited, maintained and translated into lower costs and increased productivity
- To agree the requirements for integrating current business systems to speed the creation and transfer of essential information

Basic principles

- No lowering of business standards
- Ensure staff understand the review is not an attack on numbers but an opportunity to make better use of people's abilities, time and efforts
- Involve people at all levels in identifying un-necessary information and wasteful practices
- Stop simple things becoming complicated
- Justify information or scrap it – if in doubt, the balance should be weighed in favour of elimination
- Do not legislate for exceptions by preparing or storing non-essential information 'just in case'
- We will trust our management and staff to interpret broad directives sensibly – we can then challenge current safeguards and controls
- Use sensible approximations and present essential information at the level of detail and accuracy necessary to make commonsense judgments and

decisions
- Information only given to those people who need it
- Be prepared to take some risks and encourage people to trial new ideas and implement agreed changes
- Quantify savings at all stages

Method

- Establish an informal network of people to help identify what we have now, what is required, what can be eliminated and what can be rationalized
- Review and challenge major operations and procedures, involving both producer and user
- Test proposed changes and new ideas and create model environments to hasten the spread of best practices
- Raise awareness of progress and achievements as well as stimulating action for further savings by:
  - Creating displays and exhibitions
  - Good and regular communications
  - Encouraging healthy competition to produce ideas

Success criteria

The success of the review will be judged by:
1 Reducing the volume of information and

> paperwork by an initial 25 per cent, with subsequent savings of 5 per cent per annum for three years. At the same time, cutting £10 million from the operating costs.
>
> 2 Reducing the quantity of information stored on computers and the cost of providing it.
>
> 3 Creating a questioning attitude, at every level, towards the value of all information and paperwork.

From the start it was important to guarantee that there would be no job losses as a result of the campaign. Due to a downturn in the UK economy it had been necessary to reduce the head office staff by 600 in the previous year and it was essential that people at all levels participated enthusiastically in the review without fear of talking themselves out of a job. The Marks & Spencer staff could all too readily identify with the problems caused by excess paperwork – it was part of everyone's working life. In fact many of them felt they were unable to do the important things well because non-essential paperwork was soaking up their time. They saw the attack on paperwork as a genuine opportunity to make things better for themselves on a day-to-day basis.

PHASE ONE

The review team kicked off the campaign by looking at the flow of information to the stores from various different sources: head office, the Financial Services Centre, the merchandise distribution centres and the six regional offices (see Fig. 1). It was clear that this paperwork was placing a heavy administrative burden on store staff and to quantify just how great this burden was, 12 stores were asked to list all the paperwork and information they received for a period of one month.

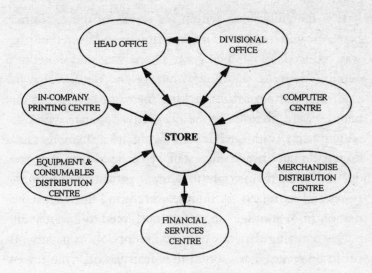

Communication to and from a Marks & Spencer store

An exhibition was set up in Baker Street to illustrate the avalanche of instructions, newsletters, pro formas, guides and telexes faced by the stores. Displays were created which showed the quantity of paper received from the various information sources along with associated costs. Store staff had already begun to question the usefulness of many documents and these were highlighted along with actions already taken to reduce the flow of paperwork. Many of the displays were created by the recipients of the information in the stores.

More than 1,000 staff were given a guided tour of the exhibition, starting with the chairman and the board who found that the scale of bureaucracy was even worse than they had previously imagined. A comment frequently heard from those attending was 'if we are like this, what are other organizations like?'

It is incredible that within six weeks of the exhibition being created the flow of information to and from the stores was reduced by 50 per cent. There was undoubtedly a genuine desire to see things improve and the fact that the chairman was personally backing the campaign meant that people were anxious to be seen to cooperate with the review team. With Sir Richard saying 'it's a shambles and a disgrace' many head office staff began to realize that they did not have a divine right to demand information from the stores and started to ask themselves 'could I find that information from another source?' or 'do I need to find it at all!'

Recognizing that this dramatic reduction in paperwork could be reversed as soon as the 'heat was off', the review team sat down with a group of store managers and the information-producers in head office to identify the minimum information needed by the stores to operate. As a result of these actions the mail from head office to the stores dropped to 25 per cent of its original level. It was discovered that much of the flow from the centre was telling people how to do things. Much of this information was common sense and, in the words of one director, 'of the teach them to suck eggs variety'. Sir Richard had emphasized that the organization employed highly paid, professional managers and they didn't need a piece of paper telling them what to do in every situation. The approach he advocated was 'Let them get on with it – if it's raining outside, they don't need to be told to put umbrellas at the front of the store.' Some of the procedure manuals disappeared overnight and others were simplified. An approach based on the Pareto principle was developed and people were encouraged to ask: 'On the 80:20 principle what are the key features here? What is the essential information? If there are 10 key points, let's make sure everyone knows what they are. On the occasions where people don't know what to do they can always ask someone.'

Three large stores, whose management had been passionate about the campaign from the start, were selected to become model environments. The store managers along with junior managers and sales assistants enthusiastically conducted a rigorous examination of all the output from their stores as well as information they generated and circulated for their own use. Spectacular reductions in photocopying, filing and computer printouts were achieved and managers from other stores were invited to come and see how these minimal paper environments operated.

One of the major successes of the review was a reduction in the avalanche of newsletters and weekly updates sent to the stores from various head office buying departments and operational areas. Previously much of this paperwork was not actioned because store personnel missed the vital information or they didn't have time to read it all. The review team worked with their colleagues in head office to condense all this information into a single document. The response from readers was far greater and the information-producers could immediately see there was greater value in the concise document.

The review team also found that the store staff were frequently distracted by ad hoc requests for information from head office. Each time such a request was made someone in each of the 300 stores had to delve out information, put it together and send it to head office where it was all collated. Upon closer examination it was discovered that in some cases the information was found to be non-essential and in others the information could have been obtained from existing systems. Furthermore, because of these frequent requests for paperwork store managers were tending to generate and retain information 'just in case' somebody senior from head office might request it. It was agreed that systems would not be created for anything other than essential information and head office staff were re-educated to accept that everything would not necessarily be already written down. If it was important to know, the store manager could find out.

An attack on unnecessary hoarding of documents meant that in-store filing was reduced by 50 per cent, an average of 44 stacks per store. The review team uncovered stacks of documents that were kept for up to five years – but never referred to! They were reliably informed that the documents had to be kept for audit or legal purposes but when the legal people were asked they didn't know the information was retained and said much of it was unnecessary anyway. They willingly reviewed all information to confirm what needed to be kept and for how long.

The review team recognized the dangers of junk paperwork migrating to electronic format. There was a feeling that at least with paper you could see it, feel it, loathe it and get rid of it, but when hidden it became a more dangerous thing. It was discovered that the equivalent of three billion sheets of paper was retained on disk throughout the organization. By highlighting what it cost to store this information, and pointing out that much of it was never accessed, the team managed to clear 70 per cent of disk storage space. The team also found that computer systems were routinely producing masses of unnecessary information. If the system was capable of producing a report, it was pulled off and people's desks were littered with 'huge piles of stuff that wasn't looked at from one week to the next'. Working with the IT people the review team achieved a reduction in computer printouts by over 12 million sheets per year. Their combined efforts meant that costs of £1.5 million were avoided.

Next the review team turned its attention to unnecessary photocopies and achieved a 40 per cent reduction. The stores' annual photocopying costs were highlighted and people were asked to send copies only to those who needed to action something. Previously many copies had been circulated for information purposes only or as a signal to the recipient that the sender was working hard.

By the end of the review 70 per cent of the mail between head office and the stores was eliminated – a weekly avalanche of 300 documents was whittled down to a more manageable 90 items. Store managers were freed to do 'real work' and 25 per cent of first line management time was released from administration to customer service. This necessitated a culture change amongst people who saw work as filling in bits of paper and not standing on the sales-floor looking for customers to serve. At around the time of the review there was a major customer care programme.

Over 500 staff were released from administrative tasks to deal directly with customers which was equivalent to an investment of £5 million in customer care. Half a million pounds' worth of desks and filing cabinets was released for new store openings. Once the furniture was removed office space was converted into salesfloor and stores were able to increase takings by an additional £500 per square foot.

PHASE TWO

Phase two of the review concentrated on simplifying the processes within the Baker Street head office and brought similarly impressive results. Each of the eight head office sections appointed a team of senior managers to coordinate the review in their area. Sir Richard Greenbury took an active interest in the review's progress and his visits to different departments specifically to focus on its results created a degree of healthy competition between them. He also attended presentations given to all levels of staff, listened to their paperwork reduction ideas and cut down his own requirements for routine information.

The six regional offices reduced administrative work by over 70 per cent and managed to eliminate 40 per cent of their standard forms from over 600 to under 450. Applying the AOR principle they reduced the outflow of information from their in-house printing centre and told information users that information was available directly from their PCs – if they needed it! As a result the equipment budget was cut by £1.5 million and the stationery budget was also reduced by over £1 million. The Food division saved 7.5 million sheets of paper per annum. The Finance

Group saved £0.6 million by eliminating 11 million sheets of paper.

The review also helped to reiterate the principle within the company that personal contact is important and that it's better to talk than to write. During the course of conversations with suppliers the Marks & Spencer staff would often be asked 'can you confirm that in writing?' but the standard response tends to be 'no, the arrangement is made unless I ring you to the contrary'. If something has to be written down and you can't say it on two sides of a piece of paper then the reaction is likely to be 'we don't want to hear it, it's too complicated'. The more senior the person the greater the insistence that your document has got to be brief, otherwise you don't make a case and it's not read.

Overall Marks & Spencer estimated the value of the review at over £50 million per annum. There was a greater focus on the customer as staff who previously thought that real work was 'paperwork' were re-educated to think that real work was standing around looking for a customer to serve. There was no loss of standards or necessary controls. The involvement of those at all levels in the organization was essential to the success of the campaign. Line management throughout the organization were involved in looking at their own work area and picking out a couple of processes and asking 'What's happening, how can we simplify it?' It encouraged people to probe what they were doing on an ongoing basis and continuous improvement has become part of the culture of the organization. The Marks & Spencer success story in conquering the information mountain can be emulated by all organizations regardless of their size or type of business.

CAMPAIGN RESULTS

In-store

- Eliminated 70 per cent of weekly mail from head office to stores (from 300 to 90 items)
- Photocopying reduced by 40 per cent
- Files and records reduced by 50 per cent (44 stacks per store)
- Computer printouts reduced by 12 million sheets per annum
- £0.75 million of furniture released for new stores
- 33 per cent of PCs redirected
- 70 per cent of disk storage space cleared out
- Converted office space to salesfloor, increasing takings by £750 per square foot
- Released 25 per cent of first line management time from administration to customer service
- 500 were redirected from administrative tasks to customer-care related activities – equivalent to an investment of £5 million in extra customercare

Regional offices

- Each office reduced administrative work by 70 per cent
- Eliminated 40 per cent of standard forms and documents (from 650 to 400 items)
- Information AOR from PCs – saving £2.3 million
- Stationery budget reduced by £1.5 million

Head office

- Food division saved 7.5 million sheets of paper per annum
- Finance group savings £1.5 million/11 million sheets of paper
- Computer services – rate of increase of stored data 30 to 5 per cent
- Internal mail reduced by 50 per cent

Overall cost savings: £50 million per annum

Also available from Random House by Declan Treacy

Clear Your Desk!

This bestselling book, which explodes the myths and excuses behind the cluttered desk, is the definitive guide to conquering the problems associated with the build-up of paperwork so common in all businesses and at all levels. It shows you how to:

- identify your paperwork problems
- reduce the inflow of unnecessary paperwork
- eliminate bureaucratic paperwork
- prioritize the paperwork allowed through
- develop a fast and efficient filing system
- systematically 'clear your desk' and keep it clear
- organize an in-company 'Clear Your Desk!' day

Declan Treacy combines his own techniques with the 'desk-clearing' secrets of top executives such as Richard Branson, Anita Roddick and Sir John Harvey-Jones. The result is a practical and proven guide to dealing with every piece of paper that lands on your desk.

Essential reading for anyone − executive and non-executive alike − who has more paperwork on the desk than time to handle it.

0 09 927192 3

Also available from Random House

Zapp!
The Lightning of Empowerment
William C. Byham Ph.D.
with Jeff Cox

ENERGIZE YOUR EMPLOYEES, BUILD UP YOUR BUSI-
NESS, AND PUT YOUR ORGANIZATION ON A HIGH-
PERFORMANCE TRACK.

Most managers know that revitalization in their companies must
occur from the ground up. But how can you get that message to
your employees without applying the kind of pressure that makes
them even less productive?

Empowerment is the answer, and it's easier to achieve than you may
think. In this motivating book you will find specific strategies
designed to help you empower your employees daily. Much more
accessible than other works on parcipitative management, Zapp!
shows you how to encourage responsibility, acknowledgement, and
creativity so that employees feel they "own" their jobs. With hands-
on examples, you will learn the basics that allow you to use this
principle in every situation, from large meetings to one-on-one
conversations to formal evaluations, and really get results.

Best of all, you can use the techniques in Zapp! to pursue any
number of business goals, whether you're trying to increase productivity, improve customer service, or innovate faster than the competition. It's all here, in an accessible guide for the successful managers
of tomorrow. Zapp! has been inspiring managers worldwide for
more than a decade. Selling 4,500,000 copies in 10 languages.

"Great fun and full of easy to use advice."
Kenneth Blanchard Ph.D.
Co-author of The One-Minute Manager

0 7126 8035 7

Also available from Random House

Manage Your Career
The definitive guide to successful job research and career change
Brian Sutton

Whether you are looking for your first job, a new job, or a whole new career, you can't afford to start your search without focused preparation and planning. To succeed in your search, you'll need a firm grasp of how the job market works today – and an informed, professional approach.

Manage Your Career is a one-stop resource that gives you all the professional guidance and advice you need to win that job. It will boost your self-confidence and help you tackle your job-search with enthusiasm, optimism and commitment.

Manage Your Career:
- **is comprehensive** – it's a genuine jobhunter's A–Z
- **is easy-to-read** – it's been specially written in a practical and accessible style to make it easy to use
- **is for everyone** – from first-time jobhunters to people facing redundancy
- **is written by an expert** – Brian Sutton is a Human Resources and outplacement professional with two decades of experience to draw on

- Planning for success
- Who's who in the job scene
- Job vacancies – how to find them and where
- Networking
- Your CV
- Winning at interviews
- Working for yourself
- Sources of information
- Handling redundancy

0 09 927228 8

Also available from Random House

CUSTOMERS.COM
Patricia B. Seybold

CUSTOMERS.COM shows you simply and clearly how you can use information technology, including the Internet, to attract and keep customers, increase sales and improve profits.

Everyone knows the prediction: the Internet will change the way business is done. And everyone has the same fear: they will fall behind their competitors and miss the boat. CUSTOMERS.COM does not offer breathless predictions – it offers practical, easy-to-understand advice and shows you how to apply it. The author, Patricia Seybold, has advised companies such as Microsoft, Hewlett-Packard, and Ernst & Young. The advice she gives in CUS-TOMERS.COM is based on solid, proven marketing principles and on real, detailed case studies of how well-known corporations like Amazon.com, Hertz, and Dell are using the Internet successfully.

CUSTOMERS.COM:
- teaches you to think in a new way about how your company interacts with your customers and other critical partners
- shows you the eight critical success factors that will turn your company into a magnet for customers
- shows you how these success factors are already being applied by others - and how you can adapt the principles to your own business
- gives you a roadmap for the pragmatic adoption of information technology that will make it easier for your customers to do business with you

0 7126 8071 3

Also available from Random House

Mobilising The Power Of What You Know
A practical guide to successful knowledge management
Paul Miller

Every day there are countless people and teams in companies work-ing on the same issues, trying to solve similar problems from scratch that someone else in the organisation has already solved. This is both an immense waste of resources, and an extraordinary opportunity. But how can this opportunity be seized?

Mobilising The Power Of What You Know is a practical handbook that for the first time shows clearly how your organisation could benefit by mobilising the power of what its people already known.

Through fascinating case studies of well-known UK, European and multi-national companies, the book provides a superb overview of current best practice and cutting-edge thinking in the new and powerful discipline of knowledge management. The contents include helpful tips and guidance from top companies. See what they have achieved so far – and learn examples to follow and pitfalls to avoid.

Paul Miller is the managing director and co-founder of TEG, and innovative UK-based communication management consultancy. He entered consultancy following career in business journalism, and consults at senior levels to multi-nationals. He has pioneered the practical use of successful knowledge management systems within companies since 1993.

0 7126 7913 8